Woodbourne Library
Washington-Centerville Public Library
Centerville, Ohio

SPECIAL MESSAGE TO READERS

THE ULVERSCROFT FOUNDATION
(registered UK charity number 264873)
was established in 1972 to provide funds for
research, diagnosis and treatment of eye diseases.
Examples of major projects funded by
the Ulverscroft Foundation are:-

- The Children's Eye Unit at Moorfields Eye Hospital, London
- The Ulverscroft Children's Eye Unit at Great Ormond Street Hospital for Sick Children
- Funding research into eye diseases and treatment at the Department of Ophthalmology, University of Leicester
- The Ulverscroft Vision Research Group, Institute of Child Health
- Twin operating theatres at the Western Ophthalmic Hospital, London
- The Chair of Ophthalmology at the Royal Australian College of Ophthalmologists

You can help further the work of the Foundation
by making a donation or leaving a legacy.
Every contribution is gratefully received. If you
would like to help support the Foundation or
require further information, please contact:

THE ULVERSCROFT FOUNDATION
The Green, Bradgate Road, Anstey
Leicester LE7 7FU, England
Tel: (0116) 236 4325

website: www.foundm

D1056532

Washington-Centerville Public Library
Centerville, Ohio

STALIN'S HAD IT NOW!

'So you lot want to be pilots? Bloody hell, Stalin's had it now!' Such were the withering words of the corporal as he eyed his raw National Service recruits. When young James Stevenson was called up in 1952, he knew exactly how he wished to serve his country — flying in the RAF. From his very first flight in a Tiger Moth ('Excuse me, sir, where are the brakes?') to mock dogfights with his fellow trainees (strictly forbidden), square-bashing and Brasso-ing in England to spinning aerobatics over the snowy prairies of Canada, this is the story of James's quest for his coveted wings.

Books by James Stevenson
Published by Ulverscroft:

DARTMOUTH CONSPIRACY

JAMES STEVENSON

◆

STALIN'S HAD IT NOW!

Learning to be a fighter pilot
during the Cold War:
Teenage Memories

Complete and Unabridged

ULVERSCROFT
Leicester

First published in Great Britain in 2014

First Large Print Edition
published 2015

The moral right of the author has been asserted

Copyright © 2014 by James Stevenson
All rights reserved

A catalogue record for this book is available
from the British Library.

ISBN 978–1–4448–2582–4

Published by
F. A. Thorpe (Publishing)
Anstey, Leicestershire

Set by Words & Graphics Ltd.
Anstey, Leicestershire
Printed and bound in Great Britain by
T. J. International Ltd., Padstow, Cornwall

This book is printed on acid-free paper

Introduction

My decision to write these memoirs was an easy one. Quite simply it is an attempt to describe what turned out to be the most exciting two years of my life. National Service was abolished long ago, but I was lucky enough to experience it and learn to fly the jet fighters of the day.

But how, you might ask, is it possible to remember all the details after 60 years? How can I include dialogue in this story when it's impossible to remember exactly what was said? Well, I can truthfully say that the odd phrase is firmly stuck inside my head but obviously I can't remember the exact words of some of the conversations that I've attempted to recreate here. But talking of memory I have to say that throughout my fourteen months as a guest of the Royal Canadian Air Force I wrote long air mail letters to my parents: fresh memories, all written at the time. Inevitably there are certain episodes that teenagers prefer not to reveal to their parents, and in my case the memory of these is vivid and needs no embellishment. When my parents died my

1

brother Hew discovered all these letters intact and was good enough to deliver them back to me; I have included nearly all of them, copied out word for word with very little editing. I also still have a hard-back notebook entitled *Royal Canadian Air Force* — *Pilot's Flying Log Book*, in which I recorded all my flights complete with their purpose and date. This log book and those letters together with photographs taken with my own camera, or else generously sent to me by RAF colleagues to whom I'm extremely grateful, have helped me to accurately describe those two exciting years.

I start the book by recounting some earlier scenes from my childhood. Why? Because those war years made a big impression on me and gave me a life-long interest in the causes and effects of warfare. I had, after all, seen and heard for myself some of the effects, if not the causes, during the 1940s.

1

I'm told that Adolph Hitler's broken promises and greedy advances into Europe forced my ill-prepared country to declare war on Germany when I was just two months short of my fifth birthday. My father, a retired naval officer, rejoined the Silent Service, caught a train from Newcastle on Tyne to Scotland on that dreadful day and disappeared from my life — two years were to elapse before I saw him again. While Daddy was in his Royal Naval ship escorting convoys of merchant ships bringing vital supplies of food to Britain, we at home quickly realised that wasting food was tantamount to betrayal. Nobody wanted to be Hitler's friend, heaven forbid.

Mother sent me to Overcliff School in Tynemouth. I walked along the seafront from Cullercoats to Tynemouth on my first day guided by my elder brother. Six weeks later a solemn school mistress entered the classroom and told us that France had fallen. I had no idea what she was talking about. How can a country fall? Where does it fall to?

On 15 August 1940, after a whole year of

wondering if I'd ever again feel Daddy's sandpaper kiss on my cheek, and thinking about those convoys of his bringing food to keep us alive, I was sitting next to his empty chair at the dining-room table at lunch during the summer holidays. Ronald was beside me with Mother sitting opposite. We didn't know it at the time but the Battle of Britain had moved briefly to our part of England, the industrial North East. Because of my instilled hatred of Hitler I was dutifully doing my bit for Britain by forcing down my lunch, but I was full. The last few spoonfuls of rice pudding remained on my plate uneaten when . . .

We heard a loud wailing sound — low-high-low-high-low. The sound of aircraft and the thud-thud-thud of anti-aircraft guns, interspersed with louder explosions of enemy bombs, rattled the French windows. My elder brother was, and still is, one of those people who do everything to perfection without delay. On this occasion (aged eight) he had already finished his pudding and asked Mother if he could take shelter under the table. This idea had been put about by the government — it was, after all, the safest place to be when ceilings and walls start collapsing. Mother smiled approval, and it didn't take a genius to know what she was thinking: *what a good boy you are, Ronnie, so bright and clever.* Her appreciative nod sent Ronald diving for safety while the clamour of war came a step closer. As I put another slimy spoonful into my mouth a flake of plaster detached itself from the ceiling, spiralled down like a sycamore seed and narrowly missed the remains of my rice pudding. 'Mother, may I go under the table too?'

The answer came quicker than the flash of an exploding bomb: 'Not until you've made a nice clean plate.'

Over a year later, on Sunday 9 November 1941 to be precise, His Majesty's Ship *Montclare* was due to arrive in a Cornish harbour for a refit and some well-earned Christmas leave for her crew. Mother lost no time. She booked rooms at the Pentargon Hotel in Falmouth and bundled her three sons, Ronald, me and Hew (aged two) onto a southbound train from Newcastle. I remember feeling nervous because after two years I'd forgotten what my father looked like. At Falmouth we had a wonderful family reunion and, once again, I was able to feel that familiar scrape of sandpaper on my cheek and the sweet smell of tobacco and gin on my father's breath at bed time.

Four days after my father's arrival at

Falmouth the British aircraft carrier HMS *Ark Royal* was sunk near Gibraltar. All the grownups were talking about it and even at my young age I sensed disaster. Britain stood alone. Most of Europe had been overrun by the enemy. However, little did we think, during our brief stay at the Pentargon, we would very soon be rejoicing at an unexpected turn of events that changed the course of the war.

Hotel life was a new experience for me. I sneaked into the billiard room to watch men from the ship trying to hit balls into holes. One of them told me that if I put a snooker ball into my mouth it would stay there until cut out by a surgeon. To this day I think back to the Pentargon every time I enter a hotel. A young maid with a strange accent taught me to tell the time with the aid of an extremely tall grandfather clock. Even at the tender age of seven I realised that Daddy and Mother needed some private time together after such a long separation, so Ronald and I were more than happy to be billeted on board HMS *Montclare* for a few days. The skeleton crew left in charge of the ship spoiled us rotten. The ship's bosun gave my brother and me a length of rope each, long enough to dangle over the side and touch the water. I managed to let my rope drop into the harbour and sink, and the following day was alarmed to see a sailor marking the place by painting a white arrow on the jetty. Only later did I discover that he was marking the spot where a box of ammunition had sunk. We were also allowed to sit behind an anti-aircraft gun and twiddle handles to aim at the many barrage balloons protecting the harbour. Ronald and I were given an officer's vacant cabin and I was surprised at how many pretty sisters that officer seemed to have judging by several photographs of young ladies on his cabin wall, some so scantily clad that I was surprised they hadn't all died of pneumonia.

On Sunday 7 December, Japanese forces made a surprise attack on American ships in Pearl Harbour, a US deep-water base in a far-away Hawaian island. For the British and Canadian crew members billeted at the hotel this news had a dramatic effect. For the first time in my short life I witnessed adults behaving like children. On Christmas day, at lunch, bowls full of paper balls were brought to each table and a battle royal ensued. Only later did I realise the reason for all the smiles and laughter. The American giant was awake at last and had declared war on Japan and Germany. At long last everybody knew that all would be well.

On Daddy's 39th birthday his ship sailed

back into the war and we didn't see him again until he arrived at our rented house in Oxford in April 1942. As the hour of his homecoming approached I noticed my mother becoming increasingly agitated and excited. Just before he was due to arrive she dashed upstairs to make herself beautiful, leaving me listening for the doorbell (my elder brother was away at boarding school). The bell rang. I froze and for some unknown reason was too scared to open the door. Here was Daddy home from the sea and here was me hesitating for so long that he had to ring the bell a second time. Mother came down the stairs three at a time, fiddled for eternal seconds with the lock, threw the door open and threw herself into Daddy's arms. He dropped his kitbag and my parents hugged each other like grizzly bears. I clung on too.

Later, after I had gone to bed, Daddy came into my bedroom and unloaded his kitbag onto the floor. I remember a growing pile of Canadian cans of butter, tinned ham, sardines, boxes of matches and many wonderful things that we desperately needed.

Becoming a training officer at the Royal Naval College in Dartmouth must have seemed like a welcome rest after escorting convoys to and fro across the U-boat infested Atlantic. A sleepy harbour town would surely be the ideal place for a weary sailor to rest and recuperate. We moved into another rented house within walking distance of the college and I was enrolled at Tower House Primary School, 200 yards from our house.

When the Naval College was on leave the pupils of Tower House were encouraged to go swimming in the college pool every Friday under the watchful eye of Petty Officer Savage. On 18 September 1942 my mother received a telephone call from the Naval College to say that swimming had been cancelled because Petty Officer Savage would be unavailable. Instead of swimming she sent me on an errand to deliver a note to the headmistress of Tower House. The note contained arrangements for me to become a boarder because Mother was soon to give birth to her fourth child whom, I later worked out, had been conceived in the Pentargon Hotel.

Walking back from school after delivering the note, hand-in-hand with my three year old brother Hew, I heard two very loud explosions. We looked down the road and saw an aircraft above the tower of St Clements Church. It was flying directly towards us. Within seconds it was skimming bungalow roofs close to where we were standing. We stood there, surprised, unable to move. I saw a black swastika and the face of a German pilot. Two RAF Spitfires were in hot pursuit with guns blazing. In a deafening roar all three aircraft cleared the tower of my school and disappeared from sight. Mother, alerted by the din, dashed out of the house. Finding us both still alive she ticked me off soundly for not throwing myself and my small brother to the ground at the sound of guns as I had been taught. That afternoon a policeman broke into the house next door. He told us that our neighbour had been killed during an attack on the College. 65 years later I received a letter from the deceased's nephew who had read about the incident in my first novel *Dartmouth Conspiracy*.

Six enemy aircraft had attacked Dartmouth. Twelve bombs had fallen on the town leaving 25 dead. How the RAF Spitfires turned up so promptly to repel this surprise attack was a question I kept asking myself. I found out the answer fifty years later when researching my novel.

Although the war ended in 1945, conscription into the armed forces of Great Britain lasted until 1960. All able-bodied males born before September 1939, who weren't employed down coal mines or on farms, had to start two years National Service at eighteen, or later if at school or university. Throughout the 1950s the Queen's conscripts were at war on several fronts notably in Korea where Chinese and Russian Communists were in conflict with the West. The first Hydrogen bomb was tested in 1951 on a remote island in the Pacific and we could only guess what would happen if it were ever used against the ever-spreading Russian grip on Europe. Two British diplomats had disappeared behind the Iron Curtain. Trouble was brewing in Egypt over the Suez Canal. Mau Mau tribesmen were murdering and mutilating colonial farmers in Kenya — so it was hardly surprising that the British Government needed a steady flow of cannon fodder in the shape of National Servicemen to defend Democracy and the remnants of a shrinking empire.

Male, born in 1934 — yes, I qualified for National Service. I prefer to think of it as my chance to apply a milligram of pressure towards the downfall of Joseph Stalin, our dodgy ally during WW2 but now publicly licking his lips at the prospect of European domination. Was I up to it? At my tough boarding public school I was an undersized washout at games and routinely caned by a sadistic housemaster for my lack of ability at French and Latin. In an effort to escape from the mind-blowing boredom of foreign grammar I decided to build a massive model glider in the school's windowless air raid shelter and, when the sadist discovered what I was doing he laughed at my efforts: 'It will never fly.' I pressed on and completed the five-foot wingspan (my height at the time) with expensive balsa wood. My plan was to attach the glider to the back of my bicycle, ride like hell across the playing fields and hope that it would rise like a kite behind me, drop the string and fly, and fly, and fly a long way to anywhere — and I didn't care if I never saw it again as long as my tormentor was there to witness the event. But I ran out of pocket money before the build was complete so Stinker was right — my glider never flew and my project ended its life in the dustbin.

Light relief, however, was at hand. Every Wednesday afternoon we were taught how to march up and down with our Lee Enfield rifles at the slope. We presented arms, ordered arms, shot blanks and cleaned our rifles because one day soon we would be asked to go and kill the enemy wearing highly polished boots, bright cap badges and carefully cleaned webbing. On Field Days we were issued with clips of blank ammunition and fought carefully planned battles over the Dorset countryside. The Combined Cadet Force stood me in good stead when I found myself enrolled in the Royal Air Force. (As for my schoolboy failure at languages, ten years after leaving school I became fluent in Spanish and Portuguese — but I learned those languages in the same way that I learned English — by ear and not from a book).

As soon as I was legally old enough I persuaded my father to take me away from School's boring routine and traumatic punishments and afterwards spent a wonderful 'gap year' on a Sussex farm before being called up for National Service. My short stay at Sheffield Mill Farm stirred something in my genes — probably inherited from my mother who was descended from a Hampshire farmer. I milked cows with names like Ada, Natty and Marigold. My employer, Bill Hunt, was an eccentric raconteur with endless stories about his army life during the war. In 1952 the dust of war had barely settled and Britain's farmers were encouraged to produce as much food as they could. The country was still restricted by food rationing and, in hungry post-war Britain, farmers were heroes.

Every morning I'd climb out of bed at some ungodly winter's hour, light my candle, go downstairs and snatch a cup of tea in the kitchen with Bill and former land girl Valerie. Stomping up the hill to the cowshed Bill would say: 'Sustain yourself with the happy thought that we are about to make an important contribution to the national breakfast. We milk cows, we collect eggs and we feed bacon pigs.' It was great — far better than shedding tears of frustration over French irregular verbs and Latin declensions. I would have gladly spent the rest of my life at Sheffield Mill Farm, teaching calves how to drink milk substitute from a bucket, cutting hay with a converted horse-drawn mower pulled behind a wheezy old Fordson tractor, taking eggs to Uckfield packing station every week and trying not to blush at the banter of girls who worked there. 'Too young sonny boy, bet you've never had your leg over.'

I soon got used to living without electricity. The earth-closet was at the end of a path behind the cottage but at last I had the dignity of earning my living — twenty shillings per week. Every Saturday night Lesley and Bill Hunt, Valerie and I would pile into a massive Austin Ten and drive to the Uckfield Picture House. One WW2 film I remember was *Appointment with Venus* starring David Niven and Glynis Johns. Halfway through the film, just as plans were being made for Venus (a valuable cow) to be smuggled out of a German occupied Channel Island, Bill nudged me. 'I forgot to switch off the Autovac.' I immediately got up, went outside, lifted one side of the Austin's bonnet and twisted a small brass tap — luckily the engine was still warm, if I had done this on a cold engine we would have been unable to start the car for the journey home.

I had a lot of fun at Sheffield Mill Farm but soon realised that profits were low and money was tight. The only way Bill could make the place pay was by taking in paying guests for cheap summer holidays. Families who lived in smoky places like Birmingham, London or Manchester enjoyed their holidays at Sheffield Mill Farm. Having read the phrase 'no aspidistras here' in Bill Hunt's advertisement, guests seemed willing to grab a rake and turn rows of cut grass during haymaking or get involved in other farming tasks. During supper we all sat round the dinner table listening to Bill's uninhibited stories about life as a junior officer in charge of a remote coastal battery in Scotland during WW2, and afterwards the fun would continue with everyone helping with washing up.

Bill's wife was a lot older than he was; it was a second marriage for both of them. Lesley was a happy person, she named her cat So Small and would feed Mrs Grundy (her pet goose) whenever she knocked on the back door for free handouts. One day on entering the pig shed I saw Bill holding Valerie (capable, young and very attractive) tightly in his arms — both so engrossed that I was able to make a quick retreat without being seen. Poor Valerie, she confided in me that she came to the farm to recover from a disastrous love affair that landed her in a blood-filled bath during a back-street abortion that left her sterile. How strange to think that, sixty years later, unwanted pregnancies can be legally terminated by qualified doctors.

Bill Hunt rented the farm from the Sheffield Park Estate owned by the Soames family. The estate gamekeeper, Mr Burley, lived in a nearby cottage. He wasn't at all burly but a rather wizened figure in gaiters with spaniel at heel and shotgun under arm. He was, as they say, a man of few words. 'You staying long at Mr Hunt's?'

'Until the autumn.'

He took a step closer. 'What then?'

'I have to do my National Service. I want to be a pilot.'

Mr Burley surveyed me for several seconds. His frown showed an extra furrow. 'Pilot is it? Trouble is you might come down quicker than you went up.' I dismissed this comment with a casual shrug but twelve months later that prophesy very nearly came true.

Throughout my time at the farm I wrote truthful letters to my parents — nothing but the truth — but not the whole truth. I never told them about my chosen form of entertainment during days-off in the seaside town of Brighton with its variety shows. I remember seeing *Naughty but Nice* and *Sunshine Sea and Exercise*. Thank you Brighton — seeing all those naked midriffs and high-kicking legs converted me into a dedicated theatre fan.

2

Queen Elizabeth the Second, as yet uncrowned, needed plenty of bright-eyed youths to protect her Empire. When war broke out in Korea (1950) the period of compulsory service in Her Majesty's armed forces was increased from eighteen months to two years. September 1952 found me reasonably fit, I wasn't blind, I wasn't mentally ill nor was I a clergyman, a coal miner or a farm labourer because I had willingly given up my protected agricultural occupation hoping to fly. So take me. Ma'am, I'm ready. I want to qualify as a pilot and be allowed to fly one of your jet fighters. I left the farm, went home and waited.

When a letter marked ON HER MAJESTY'S SERVICE dropped through our front door I tore it open and punched the air. Call-up papers at last. On the appointed day I kissed my mother goodbye, walked to Darlington, caught the bus to Middlesbrough and handed my papers to a man sitting at a table. He glanced at them, gave them back to me and pointed to a row of chairs. 'Wait over there.'

I sat down, picked up a newspaper and pretended to read.

'Stevenson. J?'

I stood up, knocked on a door and went in. An officer in crumpled khaki looked up from his desk. 'Ah, yes, Stevenson J. I'm Captain Blenkinsop. Sit down please. The British army are looking for boys like you.'

'I want to join the RAF and volunteer for aircrew.'

'AIRCREW?' He looked me up and down. 'Are you quite sure? Have you brought your School Certificate?'

After looking at it closely he continued. 'It's all very well you wanting to fly with the RAF, Stevenson, but what makes you think the Brylcreem boys will want you? That is the question, whether 'tis nobler in the mind to suffer life with those buggers or join the British army and do a proper job for Queen and Country?' I started to protest but he cut me short. 'Oh well, if you insist on impossible dreams you'll have to take the intelligence test.' He ushered me into an adjacent room, sat me behind a desk and gave me paper and pencil. 'You've got three minutes.'

I looked at the first question: If men walk and birds fly, what do fishes do? Was it a trick? I ticked the box marked swim, moved on to the next and finished all twenty questions with time to spare. Captain Blenkinsop surveyed my paper and nodded appreciatively.

'Aircrew was it? I'd better warn you that many are called but few are chosen — The Few — ever heard that phrase before?' Before I had time to answer he continued: 'The Air Ministry, quite understandably, don't want to be caught with their trousers down — meaning that too few of the Few were ready for action last time the balloon went up. I'll mark your card 'aircrew' and you'll have to make absolutely sure you get yourself into the right stream once you get to your Reception Unit. That's all. Good luck. Call in Thompson on your way out. And by the way, happy landings!' I went home without realising that the aircrew window for National Servicemen would soon be closed for good.

Several days later another brown envelope fell through the door. Somebody claiming to be my obedient servant demanded my presence at Royal Air Force Station Padgate on 2 September 1952, rail warrant enclosed. On Platform One at Darlington station I took a last look at the 100 year old railway engine *Locomotion*, kissed my mother goodbye and boarded the train for Lancashire. 'Don't forget to write. Remember to change at Crewe.' The train was crowded. Nervous youths played cards with their friends; others read *Tit-Bits* or *Reveille* and looked out of the window with dewy eyes. We were the recruits, upholders of the British Empire, lambs to the slaughter with minimal luggage. At Padgate station a man wearing a pale-blue uniform under his rain cape pointed to a camouflaged truck. 'All those joining the mob get in.'

Today that old wartime bomber station's wide areas are covered with the comfortable suburbs of Warrington, but in 1952 RAF Padgate was a bleak, unwelcoming place. We jumped down from the truck. An RAF man also wearing a waterproof cape introduced himself and called out our names from a list. 'Aircrew volunteers Norman, Norrington, Rose, Stevenson, Stewart, Simpson, Smith, Snelgrove, Tucker and Unwin are allotted to G47,' which turned out to be a hut made of curved sheets of corrugated iron containing twelve beds and a cast-iron stove. We looked at each other. There was something familiar about one of my companions. I recognised him before he recognised me. 'Hello Roger.' Norrington and I had been fellow pupils at primary school. He had made his name as a young musical prodigy at the Dragon School in Oxford and we hadn't seen each other since 1948. We shook hands rather formally while a freezing wind whistled from the gap where our ill-fitting chimney joined the corrugated roof.

None of us knew about the hazards awaiting us in the adjacent Ablutions Block. No home comforts there — every movable object had been stolen — no toilet paper, no plugs in the basins and sometimes the overhead lights (even if they had bulbs) wouldn't work because of a plundered fuse box. Fortunately we shared our ablutions with washers, shavers, shampooers and so-ons from other huts, some of them were old hands nearing the end of their three-week stint at Padgate. I was amazed to see the stuff they carried in their wash bags: a six-inch nail wrapped in an unlubricated condom worked wonders in the fusebox; a pre-decimal penny wrapped in a handkerchief exactly fitted the basin plughole.

On our first morning, having successfully survived the ablutions and registered our various religions (automatically C of E if you hesitated), Corporal O'Maley told us to: 'Get fell in' for the Clothing Parade. We marched to the store, formed a line and approached a counter marked Footwear. The sergeant in charge of boots and shoes never asked what size. After a quick glance at our feet he would shout out the size to his assistant. The recruit in front of me said, 'Excuse me I think I'm a size eight in a wide fitting, or maybe an eight and a half.' He received a withering look and got a size nine that fitted perfectly. Then it was shirts with detachable collars, black tie, vests, underpants, socks etc. The housewife airmen-for-the-use-of turned out to be nothing more than a roll of cloth tied with tapes containing needles, cotton, spare buttons and darning wool. Working Blue and Best Blue uniforms followed, the latter for use on official parades had brass buttons each with an embossed eagle soaring over a royal crown.

A large sheet of brown paper and a length of string, the last items to be drawn from stores, soon kept us busy. Dressed as Aircraftsmen Second Class we wrapped up our civilian clothes and addressed them to our various mothers. No civilian clothes meant no escape from Stalag Padgate. During free time on Saturday evening 6 September, four days after I had joined 'the mob', while polishing boots and brasses, someone turned on the hut radio.

This is the BBC Home Service, here is the news.

Nobody took any notice.

At least 27 people have been killed and 63 injured after a jet fighter disintegrated and fell into the crowd at the Farnborough Air Show in Hampshire.

Now the BBC had our full attention,

The De Havilland 110 fighter had just broken the sound barrier when it broke up over the spectators showering them with debris. Among the dead are the pilot, John Derry, and the test observer Anthony Richards. Mr Derry was the first British pilot to exceed the speed of sound in this country four years ago today in a DH 108 research aircraft.

All was silent in Hut G47.

The two airmen had completed one fly-past in which they amazed 130.000 spectators by breaking the sound barrier to produce a sonic boom. During the second low-level flypast, travelling at about 500 mph over the aerodrome, the nose lifted and the whole plane disintegrated. The two engines broke loose. One plunged into a dense crowd watching on the hillside. The other engine fell on open ground. Fire engines and ambulances arrived within minutes.

Could it really be true?

After a short break the air display continued with Squadron Leader Neville Duke, a close friend of Mr Derry, flying a Hawker hunter to a

height of 40,000 feet and then diving to create
a double sonic boom.

The John Derrys and Neville Dukes of
the future kept on spitting, polishing and
staying calm. I remember sitting down to
my plate of stew in the camp mess hall that
evening feeling more determined than ever
to sit in the cockpit of a De Havilland jet
and dive it through and beyond the deadly
barrier.

'Get fell in, tallest on the right, shortest on
the left.' We scrambled into line wearing our
Best Blues for Sunday Church Parade. Corporal O'Maley, while inspecting us, paused for
several seconds in front of Stewart who was
standing next to me.

'CAN YOU SHIT UPSIDE DOWN,
LADDIE?'

Stewart took a full two seconds to consider
the possibility. 'No.'

'No WHAT?'

'No, I can't shit upside down.'

O'Maley pointed to the rank badge on his
sleeve. 'What do you think this is, a laundry
mark? Answer the question.'

'CORPORAL, I can't shit upside down,
CORPORAL.'

He stabbed a finger at one of Stewart's
buttons. 'Neither can that f***** bird. Sew

it on the right way up or I'll have your balls for breakfast.'

O'Maley again: 'Ahhh-ten-shun. Jews and Roman Catholics take one step to the rear MOVE. The rest of you, look lively, close up. Riiight-turn, Quiiick march, left, right, left right, left right.' I marched to church with the majority and prayed for the souls of the infidels left behind. I also prayed to survive electrocution in the ablution block and — please God, help me to become a jet pilot.

Some unseen body in the Air Ministry had calculated that recruits taller than six foot three didn't fit the system; mass producing uniforms for beanpoles was obviously a scandalous waste of tax payers' money. Oversized freaks didn't fit the system, so why should the system fit them? Oh no, we don't send them home, we send for the tailor. I clearly remember Tiny Tomlinson marching up and down, like a condemned factory chimney in his tweed jacket and the longest grey flannels in the world, towering over pygmies in pale blue uniforms being sworn at by a diminutive corporal.

For three endless days during that bleak September of 1952 we shivered, we were damp and everybody was snivelling and coughing — not a good thing because we weren't allowed to take our Flying Aptitude Tests if we had

26

colds. Believing that some extra coal for the stove might be good for our health, I hit on a brilliant idea that was quickly approved by the rest of Hut G47. Raiders were selected by the short-straw method. Armed with buckets, and under cover of darkness, the giant heap of coal outside the cookhouse was plundered on a nightly basis. The results were literally incandescent. Nobody knew the melting point of iron but we must have come pretty close to it because we stoked our stove until the chimney glowed cherry-red halfway to the ceiling.

Soon after I joined the RAF, recruits were invited to volunteer for an experiment, one that might lead to an all-time cure for the common cold, this to be carried out at a place called Porton Down in Wiltshire. Luckily for me, Aircrew Volunteers were advised not to get involved in this trial as it would delay the start of our selection process. Other recruits saw it as a cushy option with no drill or physical training for at least a month, and no health problems apart from a runny nose. The experiment also involved civilian volunteers, providing them with some extra cash. At the time none of the volunteers realised that this trial had nothing to do with the common cold, but everything to do with chemical warfare. Years later I read about twenty-year-old Leading Aircraftsman Ronald

Maddison who died at Porton Down within twenty-four hours of being exposed to the nerve agent Sarin. The inquest, held in secret, concluded that Maddison had died from choking. In the years that followed many Porton Down human guinea pigs suffered lung and kidney trouble, cancer and psychological problems. In 2001 the government carried out a survey into the health of all 20,000 volunteers and seven years later issued this statement: *The government sincerely apologises to those who may have been affected.* Compensation of £8,300 was paid to each of the 369 individuals still suffering from long-term ill health before the matter was closed but further complaints from survivors re-opened the floodgates of truth and in 2004 a second inquest found that Ronald Maddison had been unlawfully killed at the hands of the State by a nerve agent in a non-therapeutic experiment.

If I live to be a hundred I don't suppose I'll ever hear a comment shouted with such venomous sarcasm: 'So you lot want to be pilots? Bloody hell, Stalin's had it now!' Followed by, 'Stevenson, you're marching about like a little wet cabbage leaf.' One day I absent mindedly turned right when everybody else turned left and O'Maley nearly blew a fuse: 'Next time you decide to go to the lavatory, Stevenson, kindly let me know and I'LL COME AND WIPE YOUR ARSE.'

By now we had each been issued with a Lee Enfield rifle and were taught to respond to yelled commands: *Slope Arms, Present Arms, Order Arms*. I knew something about this already; at school we would dress up as soldiers every Wednesday afternoon, learn how to march up and down and how best to kill the enemy. The Lee Enfield .303 rifle, made of metal and wood and invented in 1895, weighed seven pounds and was an essential part of our drill but when I joined the RAF there was one command I hadn't come across before. Our corporal told us how to do it. He stood in front of the flight and went through the movements explaining as he went. 'Now watch me closely. On the command shoulder arms, I move my left arm across the front of my body and grab the rifle with a full round grasp like so. Now I lift the rifle to the right side of the body and support its weight by inserting the middle finger of my right hand through the trigger guard. Got it? Now I return the left arm to my left side keeping the rifle vertical and close to the body at all times. Rhythm is the secret — keep the rhythm and everybody moves together in one superb short, sharp, shit-hot shuffle.' He then gave us the command and we attempted to do what we had just been shown. 'That was terrible, we'll do it again. Shoulder Arms. Come on, come on you horrible little men. You all know how to do it. Lift the rifle. Find it, find it, insert your Saturday-night finger into the trigger guard. Come on, what's the matter with you lot, look to your front, find it, find it. If it had hairs round it you'd find it quick enough.'

At mealtimes we stood in queues at the cookhouse door, each with our personal RAF issue mug-and-irons. Stew and spuds were plentifully slapped onto our plates in a heap. Washing up, if you can call it that, consisted of swishing the aforesaid mug and irons in a stainless steel trough on leaving the cookhouse — no mops or detergents. The water was kept at boiling point so if you let go of your precious irons or mug, that was that. Replacements were available, but at a price.

At every meal the duty officer of the day, known as the Orderly Officer, would make his rounds accompanied by the airmen's Mess Sergeant. The officer would walk between the tables saying, 'Any complaints, any complaints?' One day a recruit looked up at the Flight Lieutenant and made some casual comment about a black mark on his potato. The response was a high-pitched scream: 'Stand up when you address an officer!' The

30

recruit stood up, incoherent with fright. 'There is absolutely nothing wrong with those potatoes and don't you dare complain to me again.'

In a way I was sorry to leave Padgate with its screaming corporals and lonely Avro Lancaster bomber parked out in the open on a decaying runway at a time when everyone seemed to have forgotten the 55,573 men of Bomber Command who were sacrificed to keep us safe. How strange to think that when I was at RAF Padgate, seven years after the end of WW2, Britain was in a another kind of war, this time against Communism. The Western World seemed to be teetering on the brink of a major showdown with Russia.

Rules decreed that all new recruits hoping for aircrew training must first be subjected to a series of flying aptitude tests. The Royal Air Force station at Hornchurch in Essex, famous as a Fighter Command base during the war against Hitler, had been set up for the purpose. To get there we boarded the train and once again changed at Crewe with twelve minutes to spare before our connection south. We crowded into the buffet for a much-needed bun and cup of tea. Stewart was at the front of the queue and received a request from someone further back: 'Make mine a cuppa and a wad.' Everyone took up the idea and

Stewart was bombarded with orders until finally in desperation he yelled, 'What do you think I am, a bleeding octopus?'

'Left right, left right, pick up your feet you horrible little men. So you want to be pilots, eh? Thank Christ we've got a navy,' For a moment I thought that Corporal O'Maley had somehow followed us to the Aircrew Selection Centre to conduct our early-morning warm-up drill. While obediently picking up my feet, swinging my arms and turning left and right, I tried to imagine what this Essex airfield might have been like back in 1940 when it was home to Spitfire squadrons protecting London. Unlikely as it may seem, an elderly mongrel bitch called Minnie helped to recreate the scene. Rumour had it that this faithful little dog would endlessly whine for her master while he was aloft in his Spitfire — and here she was ten years later causing everybody a lot of fun by trotting in front of the column as we marched up and down the parade ground. When the order came, 'ABOUT TURN' Minnie, finding herself at the back of the column, would scamper between our stamping feet to emerge once again at the front. 'ABOUT TURN,' Scamper, scamper, and so it went on. We were having so much fun that I began to wonder if this really was the make-or-break place that would decide my future in the RAF. I didn't have long to wait.

I dropped my trousers and pulled down my underpants. 'Ever had a hernia, Stevenson?' Before I had time to reply the doctor shoved two fingers into my groin, looked at the ceiling and told me to cough. I coughed, he nodded and shouted, 'NEXT.'

A chap called Smith from Glasgow was directly ahead of me in the alphabetical queue for Nose and Throat. 'Open your mouth, Smith, and stick out your tongue.' The doctor shoved his wooden spatula so far down Smith's throat that the poor chap almost threw up. 'Control yourself man.' The spatula probed again. Smith retched again. 'Pull yourself together. I haven't got all day.' The doctor kept on and finally had to give up. 'NEXT.' I stepped forward thinking that the unknown condition of Smith's throat might give Joseph Stalin an unfair advantage in the World War that was about to happen.

The next test proved that my eardrums weren't perforated. A surprising number of our group did have perforated eardrums and were immediately thrown off the aircrew list and un-consoled to hear that Russian pilots were rumoured to have their eardrums deliberately punctured to facilitate the equalisation of pressure while in flight. While still trying to understand the science of air

33

pressure on eardrums a solemn woman searched my hands for evidence of bitten fingernails.

A series of fairground sideshows followed. I sat down, grabbed a steering wheel and tried to keep a metal pointer in the centre of a wiggly road on a revolving drum. I sat in front of a screen, feet on a rudder bar and right hand holding a control column while attempting to keep a wandering light within a narrow square on the screen in front of me. After that I donned a pair of earphones and tried to identify bleeps — same or different — against a roar of static. At the Finger Dexterity Test the sergeant in charge explained: 'The wooden board in front of you has 48 square pegs fitted into 48 square holes. As you can see the pegs are painted white on one side and black on the other. When I say GO, grab the first peg, pull it out, twist it through 180 degrees and put it back in the hole. Carry on turning pegs until I say STOP. Any man achieving the impossible by turning every peg within the allotted time will receive a loving kiss from me upon his naked arse. Any questions? GO.' A chap called Spedding was soon sitting back with his arms folded while everybody else was still struggling. I'll never forget the look on the sergeant's face and needless to say his rash promise was quickly forgotten. Afterwards we crowded round the champion to hear that he'd spent the past six months packing biscuits of assorted sizes into tins in a Carlisle biscuit factory.

At the final interview I was faced by a boot-faced panel of doctors and officers. 'What made you volunteer for aircrew? Do you have the ability? Are you the type we're looking for?' Undaunted I described my passion for model aeroplanes, and — yes, yes — my overriding waking and sleeping ambition was to become an RAF pilot and fly the De Havilland Vampire or the twin-engine Gloster Meteor.

3

Next came the real thing, but it was a greatly diminished group that arrived at RAF Digby. There was nothing wrong with our ears, eyes okay, no hernias, no piles, bowels fine, kidneys tip-top and good blood pressure.

Airfields need flat ground and Lincolnshire had lots of it, so flat that all the county's various airfields relied on water stored in raised tanks supported at each corner by miniature Eiffel towers. These presented a hazard to low-flying aircraft and, for a different reason, caused us some trouble later on.

Humiliation was an essential ingredient in the training of Her Majesty's fighting men. Very soon we were being chivvied and made to jump to it by yet more corporal drill-instructors on yet another parade ground where they kept us busy in between lectures. But what about flying? Good old English weather was reliably bleak. When it wasn't raining the sky was opaque and milky-grey and not a sound was heard from the thirty or so De Havilland Tiger Moth biplanes that we were itching to get our hands on. The third day, however, was a lot brighter. A Tiger Moth hummed low over the parade ground and we all looked up to see a two-fingered salute delivered by a man in the rear cockpit. Seeing us all gaping at the sky brought our corporal close to hysteria. 'All right, all right, look to your front — it's one of ours.'

Tiger Moths are biplanes with open-cockpits designed in the 1930s. Those at No.1 Grading Unit Digby belonged to a civilian company called Airwork, whose instructors were under contract to sort the wheat from the chaff. The Clean Air Act of 1956 was still four years in the future so the chances of a blue sky, if not remote, were certainly few and far between. Rules, however, are rules — and 12 hours of flying in a real aeroplane would decide if a starry-eyed hopeful might one day become a proficient jet pilot capable of joining the Korean War or any other conflict that might threaten the wide frontiers of the British Empire.

We queued to draw special clothing suitable for open-cockpit flying. A bulky pair of overalls stuffed with eiderdown called a teddy bear went over your working blue battledress; another pair of overalls made of windproof and fireproof canvas went over the top of the teddy bear; shin-length suede boots lined with lamb's wool for your feet, silk gloves covered by elbow-length leather

37

gauntlets on your hands and finally a WW2 issue leather helmet with inset earphones and a pair of vintage Mark VIII goggles. Next came your means of escape from a burning aircraft, tightly attached to your bottom and individually fitted in the parachute department by a cheery group of cheeky females. 'Are you going to make those straps between your legs nice and tight or shall I do it for you? Shoulder straps next, that's it, nice and tight, be careful when you stand up or you'll be joining the WAAF choir.'

The programme was simple: half a day in ground school, the other half on flights. During a lecture on Principles of Flight one of our ground instructors, Flight Lieutenant Halcro, gave a graphic description of how his Spitfire was set upon by fighters during WW2. 'Fortunately for me,' said Halcro, 'by reducing my airspeed I was able to turn tighter than my attackers making it impossible for them to point their guns at me. The fact that my attackers were our brave allies from America surprised me somewhat.' I remember Halcro telling us that in a future war aerial warfare would be conducted by remote control. 'Even if you're shot down you'll still be able to end the day with a nice cup of tea in the mess.'

On 15 October 1952, Mr Jeffery, one of the

Airwork pilots, decided to take me up for my first flight in spite of murky 'clag' hanging over the airfield and surrounding countryside. I walked behind him, parachute over my shoulder and wet grass turning my new suede flying boots to dark brown. The shape of a yellow biplane showed dimly through the mist. 'Ever flown before, Stevenson?' I hadn't. In those days foreign holidays were almost unheard of. We walked round the aeroplane and he showed me where it was safe to step onto the lower wing. 'Be careful when you climb in, Stevenson, if you put your foot in the wrong place it'll go straight through the fabric.' I dutifully put my foot onto a narrow reinforced area marked STEP, dumped my parachute on the seat, got in, sat on the parachute and did up the straps. Mr Jeffery explained about the Sutton Harness: two more straps between your legs and another over each shoulder. He plugged the lead of my headset into a socket, so that we could talk to each other in flight, and climbed into the front cockpit. His voice crackled in my earphones. 'Remember what I told you: right hand on the control column, left hand on the throttle. Dual controls mean that everything in your cockpit is exactly the same as in mine. When I move my control column, yours will move in sympathy and so will the rudder pedals and the throttle.'

'Excuse me sir, where are the brakes?'

He laughed. 'What do you think this is, a Vampire?' The very mention of that RAF jet fighter made me ask myself, yet again, if I could ever hope to be entrusted with one. While trying not to think about French irregular verbs as a schoolboy I had frequently dreamed myself into the cockpit of a real aeroplane and now it was happening. I looked around the tiny space, a control column was between my legs, a bulky magnetic compass level with my chest and four large dials under discs of glass on the dashboard. Jeffrey waggled his control column. Mine waggled in sympathy. When he pulled it back sharply I received a blow to the groin that almost gave me the hernia that RAF pilots weren't supposed to have. I saw him reach out of the cockpit with a gloved hand to check two brass switches mounted on the outside of the fuselage and heard him shout at the attendant airman. 'SWITCHES OFF.' The airman raised his left arm, grabbed the top blade of the propeller and waited for the command. 'SUCK IN.' The airman flicked the prop clockwise through two half-turns. 'CONTACT.' Anti-clockwise, smartly down — once, twice, three times, four — BANG. The engine spluttered and settled to a steady roar.

Earlier that year I had passed my driving test and I have to say that my father's lumbering Rover never shook or vibrated like this when the engine started. The Rover also had brakes on all four wheels and a fuel gauge on the dashboard. The Tiger Moth, by comparison, had two wheels and a tail-skid, no brakes and a tiny float that slid up and down inside a glass tube attached to a fifteen gallon petrol tank set between the upper wings. A hot wind from the propeller whistled round my flying helmet. 'CHOCKS AWAY.' The airman ducked under the wing, the engine roared, the smelly wind increased to gale force and we rocked and bumped over uneven grass. While trundling to the far end of the field Mr Jeffrey continued his running commentary. 'I'm now going to turn the aircraft to face the wind for take-off. Put your hands lightly on the controls and follow what I'm doing.'

I was in a trance, and yet every detail of what followed is with me now: wind in my face, adrenalin pumping, everything shaking and then, suddenly lifting into fog, the thickest I'd ever seen and flying blind with a freezing gale pressing my goggles against my face.

'Bloody weather, Stevenson, shouldn't be flying in these conditions. But what the hell, if we keep climbing the sun will shine.'

Sure enough the fog was becoming thinner and paler. A yellow disc above was getting stronger and lighter — and — and — we burst into a land of snowy mountain tops and dazzling light that made me blink.

'Bloody, bloody, English weather.' Jeffrey was in my earphones again but I was speechless at the sight of my surroundings. We continued to climb. The sea of cloud dropped far below and resolved into a straight white line that stretched all around us as far as the eye could see. 'That's the horizon, Stevenson, it's very important for pilots. Take a good look at it.'

A tiny engine driving a wooden propeller had lifted us into a place where the sun had been shining uninterrupted, every day, for countless millions of years. 'Keep your right hand on the control column and your left hand on the throttle. Try to fix in your mind everything I do.' We did a turn to port with the controls moving in my hands and the rudder pedals making tiny movements under the soles of my fleecy boots. We did a turn to starboard and then — 'You have control, Stevenson.' Jeffrey held both his gloved hands above his head to show me what he meant. 'Try a turn to starboard and watch that horizon. Don't lose height. You're losing height. More throttle. Don't worry about it.

You have to start somewhere. I have control.'

We flew to a place where a large window in the cloud floor showed a patchwork of gloomy fields far below. We nosed down towards it with freezing wind battering my face. 'This is how we loop the loop, Stevenson, keep your hands clear. I have control.' We went into a dive. Pulling out of it my hands felt heavy in my lap, my cheeks drooped. Curving upwards again all I could see was the dazzling sky. 'Tip your head back and watch the horizon coming up behind you.' And there it was sliding up, brown and green with curving roads and an upside-down church.

We flew back to Digby hopping over treetops under a low ceiling of cloud. 'Always remember to land into wind, Stevenson. A headwind helps to prevent stalling on the approach.' We bumped down and taxied towards the hangars. As we climbed down our attendant airman said to Mr Jeffrey, 'What was it like, sir?' Jeffrey barely looked at him. 'Bloody awful!' Luckily the question referred to IT rather than ME, and if that was bloody awful I couldn't imagine what bloody good would be like.

The Signal Square was a small area in the corner of every airfield. It contained visual signals, useful for pilots flying with no radio.

Prominent in the square was a large white cruciform mounted on a swivel and, when correctly positioned, it represented an aeroplane facing into wind for landing. Pilots were supposed to check out the square as they joined the circuit but, needless to say, signal squares were seldom exactly right because the wind has a habit of changing direction without warning — thus an inexperienced pilot might line up with the cross only to find himself crabbing sideways across the grass and then risking a flip-over on landing.

Near the end of my third flight with Jeffrey he said, 'You have control, Stevenson. Take her in and land into wind.' I looked down at the signal square, lined up with the cross and closed the throttle. As we glided lower I was aware that we were drifting sideways. The aeroplane was pointing one way but we were travelling in another, it was a bit like skidding sideways in a car so, without saying anything to my instructor, I did what I thought was obvious — kept turning the Tiger Moth until we were travelling in a straight line. At the last minute Jeffrey took over with a burst of throttle. I was too high and too slow to make a safe landing and I was expecting some adverse comment. Instead he was full of praise. 'You turned into wind in spite of the signal square being wrong — not many

44

beginners do that without being told. Are you sure you've never flown before?' He told me that I was a natural pilot and would make that clear in my report. Suitably bolstered with this unexpected praise I hoped to be allowed to fly solo before my twelve hours of assessment was up.

In the two-week window of clear weather that followed I flew with Mr Jeffrey every day until finally on the 31 October 1952, I made my last flight to complete the statutory twelve hours behind a very silent and senior Mr Bale. While taking off and landing, taking off again, landing again, I was willing him to let me fly solo, but it wasn't to be, and perhaps just as well as I was hopeless at poking my head over the side of the aeroplane to accurately judge my height above a blurry green of speeding grass. My supervised landings were bumpy and dangerous but in spite of these shortcomings I had evidently done enough to convince Mr Bale that I was, after all, pilot material and worthy of going on to the next stage of training.

4

After leaving Digby, the successful ones from our diminishing group were posted on to the next stage, an intensive course of official bullying, classroom training and tests. It meant saying goodbye to a lot of new-found friends. We arrived at RAF Kirton-in-Lindsay after a short drive in the back of an RAF lorry and it was late evening by the time we'd had supper and found our billet, a large first-floor room with rows of double-decker bunks on either side of a central corridor.

Corporal Reames stood in the doorway and introduced himself. 'Lights out at eleven sharp so pull your fingers out!'

I laid my three 'biscuits' on a top-deck bunk to make a mattress, unpacked my kitbag, managed to stow most of my stuff in my locker, and was in the process of unfolding my regulation blankets when — *phut* — someone far away pulled the main switch. After some fairly ripe but futile protest we completed our bed-making and ablutions by the light of matches and cigarette lighters.

Tidiness, cleanliness, everything shiny-bright at all times was the order of the day. The wise and wonderful Corporal Reames had a habit of calling, 'Kit inspection in ten minutes,' after a busy day of lessons and drill just as we were settling down to a nice quiet evening of polish-polish-polish or maybe an exciting game of solo whist. Kit inspection meant scrambling like fighter pilots called to action: knife, fork, spoon, mug, housewife, underpants, socks, vest, webbing belt, best blue uniform, pyjamas, shoe brushes, shaving gear — the list was endless. Every item of equipment entrusted to us by the Queen had to be laid out on the bed in a set pattern and in the right order. Official kit inspections were conducted by a Flight Lieutenant closely accompanied by the dreaded Reames and woe betide any cadet whose kit was untidy or missing a spare vest or tin of polish. Each cadet had a locker for stowing his personal stuff and when my locker was opened during our first officer's inspection the Flight Lieutenant took a step back but Corporal Reames stood firm. He put his face so close to mine that I could smell shaving soap. 'HAS THERE BEEN AN EXPLOSION IN 'ERE?'

Barely had we settled into Kirton when all cadets were summoned to the camp cinema. The Commanding Officer stood in front of the silver screen, a short man with medals on chest and gold oak leaves on hat. 'Gentlemen

— if I can call you that — an act of treason was perpetrated at RAF Digby while you lot were stationed there. Person or persons unknown, and I'm talking about you lot sitting in front of me now, saw fit to climb one of the water towers at Digby and write JOE FOR KING in huge letters on top of the tank. I don't have to remind you that this is an extremely serious offence and one that has caused me considerable embarrassment. A visiting Air Vice Marshall spotted this traitorous message from the air last week and nearly had a heart attack. Now I have, and always have had, a sense of humour — BUT IF THAT GRAFFITI IS STILL THERE BY SATURDAY MORNING I WILL THROW EVERY MAN JACK OF YOU OFF THIS COURSE.'

The accusation came as a complete surprise to everybody. None of us had seen the offending words from the air but as we were the latest arrivals from Digby we were the obvious suspects, and the ones who would have to put things right or else. After the CO had left I kept my head down while Corporal Reames named three volunteers by the you-you-and-you method. The elected trio walked twenty-nine miles to Digby, climbed the water tower with brushes and black paint, obliterated the offending message and spent that night in Digby's guardroom cells. The true perpetrators were never discovered.

Polish, polish, polish — brass, linoleum and boots. Talking of boots — Golden Rule number two was never to allow the metal studs in your boots to touch, scrape or score RAF linoleum. A pile of boot-size rectangles cut from old carpets were stacked ready at the entrance of each billet to be used like skates, one under each foot. Slide, slide, slide to your bed-space, in fact slide, slide slide wherever you went. It kept the floor shining like glass. Friday evenings were set aside for scrubbing out the ablutions, putting more polish on the floor, cleaning windows, in fact cleaning everything in sight. The official name for this was Domestic Evening. While busy with our chores the chant would go up: 'Friday night is bullshit night, roll on 1954'. I firmly believe that one or two of us were hoping that within those two years Britain would be at war with Russia and that all this training and toughening-up would be put to good use.

For me those early weeks in the RAF were not unlike my years at an English boarding school (apart from the fact that if a superior rank in the RAF were to strike anyone of junior rank with fist or stick he would be court-martialled). Talking of rank, we were now Officer Cadets. Apart from subjects connected directly with flying like navigation, engineering, meteorology etc, Royal Air Force officers were expected to be leaders of men, good at public speaking and well-versed in current affairs. Every cadet was required to stand up and address the other members of his class for at least ten minutes on a prepared subject of his own choice. Coming from a family of naval officers (my father, both grandfathers, an uncle, my brother and three cousins) I decided to tell the story of HMS *Amethyst*'s daring action in the Yangtse River in 1949. Sailing upriver to deliver vital supplies to the British Embassy in Nanking, the ship was fired on by Chinese rebels and temporarily disabled. After secretly carrying out repairs unseen from the shore, *Amethyst* raised steam and, under heavy fire, made a successful dash for the open sea. Aged fourteen I vividly remember my father receiving a celebratory telegram from Uncle John: *AMETHYST* REJOINS FLEET STOP THREE CHEERS FOR THE NAVY. The *Amethyst* story became better known six years later thanks to a British film called *The Yangtse Incident*.

Jones liked to turn in early. He'd get all his kit ready for the morning, put on his

RAF-issue pyjamas, climb into bed and be fast asleep in spite of rowdy singing and noisy goings-on all around him. Seeing him blissfully sleeping was hard to resist. One evening I suggested that all of us (except Jones of course) should pretend it was morning, queue for the ablutions, put on our uniforms then give him a shake and tell him he'd be late on parade if he didn't get cracking. Jones woke up and looked at his watch — blimey, seven o'clock. He leapt out of bed and it took several minutes before he realised it was a leg-pull.

Most of our free time was spent cleaning and polishing. Even now, sixty years on, the merest whiff of Brasso or sniff of Kiwi boot polish transports me back to 1952. Brass belt buckles, cap badges, buttons — rub, rub, rub. Boots were the worst — when new from the stores the toe caps were all bubbly and pimply (I swear it was deliberate) but after rub, rub, rub and copious volumes of saliva (literally) and carefully applied layers of Kiwi mixed with the correct dose of spit the bobbles would miraculously transform themselves into an ebony-smooth finish equal to the finest patent leather. Webbing belts needed Blanco purchased from the NAAFI: scrub, scrub, scrub with a nailbrush. My education (if you can call it that) at an

English public school meant that I was already hardened to prison life, unlike some of my new friends to whom folding blankets and bedding for inspection was something they had to learn from scratch. Applying Blanco to webbing was another thing I already knew about. Stewpot used to spread Blanco on his belt like icing on a wedding cake. When thickly applied, however, Blanco dries to an inflexible crust that comes off in flakes when the belt is bent around the waist. I felt sorry for Stewpot being constantly sworn at so I took him under my wing and taught him how to do it — plenty of water, not too much Blanco and hey presto. Stewart soon got the hang of it and finally the corporals left him alone.

The RAF had satisfied itself that, in theory, I had 'Flying Aptitude' — but was I officer material? A ginger-haired Flight Lieutenant put it to me like this: 'Picture the scene, Stevenson. You've bailed out of your blazing Vampire, parachuted into the midst of a tussle between our brown-jobs and Stalin's lot. A hairy-arsed sergeant, old enough to be your uncle, grips you by the shoulder and says, 'Thank Christ for an officer. Our CO is dead. Tell us what to do.' How would you react in a situation like that, Stevenson? Would you be up to it? It's all very well being able to aviate around the sky on a sunny afternoon but nowadays RAF pilots are officers, and officers must know how to lead men in a crisis.'

Officer Cadets were also required to keep up-to-date at all times on news and current affairs. We were made to keep diaries in which we recorded our own particular slant on all major news items of the day as heard on the radio or gleaned from newspapers. I obediently wrote my entries in RAF document A452, a hardback exercise book. Once a week the ginger-haired Flight Lieutenant collected up these books, read them and added his comments in red crayon. Over successive evening, while helping Stewart with his Blanco, I listened to the BBC news about Derek Bentley and Christopher Craig, two youths who had been cornered by police while burgling a warehouse in Croydon. Sixteen-year-old Craig was accused of shooting and killing a policeman with a stolen pistol while being egged on by nineteen-year-old Bentley who was heard to shout: 'Let him have it Chris.' The trial lasted three days. Under-age Craig escaped the gallows but his unarmed accomplice was condemned to hang even though he was under arrest when the shooting took place. Those fateful words: *let him have it Chris* — what did they mean?

Bentley's barrister tried to convince the jury that he was pleading with his sixteen-year old accomplice to hand over the gun, but to no avail. The vision of Bentley standing on the trapdoor, hooded, noose around neck and hearing the priest's final blessing before the floor fell from under his feet made me angry — and I made an entry to that effect in my diary. Long after leaving the Royal Air Force I was glad when the repentant Craig was released from his cell after ten years, and gladder still when Bentley was posthumously pardoned in 1993.

Apart from parade-ground drill, jumping off high walls without breaking bones, polishing, saluting and hoping — we learned about some of the things that brown jobs are expected to do, including an all-night exercise. RAF men refer to soldiers as brown jobs because they dress in brown and spend a lot of time crawling about in brown mud. Although I had suffered some harsh punishment at school, I couldn't imagine myself enduring 24 hours without sleep. I needn't have worried. It was cold, so cold that my secret bottle of rum had no effect. At some point, while waiting patiently for the enemy to attack, I saw one of our number slink down a moonlit path and knock on the door of a remote house. Thinking that he must have forgotten to fill his water bottle I thought nothing of it, but when still absent after an hour I thought it might be wise to get him out of there before one of our NCOs or officers discovered that he was missing. Accompanied by Wilkinson I approached the house and knocked politely. An attractive blonde in her twenties opened the door while adjusting the front of her blouse. I asked her, 'Have you got one of our blokes in there?' She shook her head, stepped back and closed the door. Seconds later another door slammed and I heard boots beating a hasty retreat at the back of the house.

What made this different from playing soldiers in my school's Cadet Corps was the fact that we were actually being paid to do it. During Pay Parade we lined up in alphabetical order, stepped forward, saluted and showed our twelve-fifties (identity cards) when our names were called. We received just over one pound per week, more than enough to buy buns and tea at the Church Army or NAAFI, drink beer at less than one shilling a pint and attend dances in the local town. Civilian dances were held every Saturday night in the old Corn Exchange building in Grantham where we could meet women — we always referred to them as women, never girls. Going to town by bus we were conspicuous in our uniforms. At the Corn Hall we paid two shillings each and received an inky stamp on the wrist to be shown on re-entry, useful if you were planning a kiss in the dark before the dance was over. Women would sit in a row on one side of the hall while men stood on the other side, eyeing up the talent and making chauvinist comments. 'She looks alright, wouldn't chuck her out of bed — but how about that blonde piece sitting next to her?' 'Too thin, I like my women well-covered, imagine trying to poke a bean-pole. Ah, now there's one I wouldn't mind getting my hands on, watch this.'

I envied most of my friends who seemed more at ease with women than I was and able to take their pick without rejection. I remember walking across the wide floor of the Corn Exchange aiming for a girl that took my fancy. When she saw me coming she deliberately looked the other way so I had to stand there, in front of her, until I had her full attention. 'May I have the pleasure of this dance?' She looked at my shoes, ankles, knees, crotch, stomach and finally my face before rolling her eyes heavenward and rejecting me with a single word. This was discouraging but, rather than endure the shame of walking back empty-handed, I took one step to the left and asked the next girl. I swear she was the ugliest in the room but I was praying she'd say yes, which she did — and I was glad. She had plenty to say while we danced and when I bought her an orange juice she told me all about her brother doing National Service in Korea. It must have been that experience in Grantham Corn Exchange that set me thinking that beautiful women are so used to repelling unwanted admirers that many seem to live behind some kind of man-repelling barrier.

By the end of the course I still felt awkward dancing in the Corn Exchange, but at least I knew a lot more about how to kill the enemies of the Crown. I could shoot a pistol and hit the target at ten yards (unreliably). I had unravelled the mysteries of the Dalton Computer (not a computer as we know it today but a complicated 1940's circular slide rule used by air navigators). I knew something about aero-engines (in-line, radial or horizontally-opposed) and understood the mysterious forces that enable aeroplanes to defy gravity.

After final exams a list went up on the notice board. I pushed into the crowd hoping against hope that my name would be there. Less than half of us were listed. Names of successful candidates appeared in three columns headed Britain, Rhodesia and

Canada. I can't describe how relieved I was to find my name under Canada. I had made it and was about to be promoted to Acting Pilot Officer on Probation, widely considered by Brown Jobs and the Royal Navy to be the lowest form of human life. I liked the word Pilot but Acting and Probation made me realise that my ambition to fly one of the Queen's jets was still a long way off and might never happen.

After that things happened quickly. Officers wore tailor-made uniforms and they had bank accounts. I opened an account at Glynn Mills in London and proudly credited it with my clothing allowance voucher, a massive (in those days) £100. My naval officer father, who initially had looked on my ambition to join the RAF with some unease, insisted that I buy my uniform from Gieves of Bond Street (a traditional, which-side-do-you-dress, out-fitters) and ask for the services of Mr Errett the tailor and Mr Booth the cutter.

Every Acting Pilot officer on Probation (APO) sent to Canada needed two sets of uniform with Pilot Officer's stripe on shoulder and sleeve — khaki drill for summer, pale-blue for winter and shirts to match. Cap, gloves, rain coat etc, etc — how it all fitted into my brand new and recently invented Revelation light-weight expandable suitcase I shall never know, but fit it did. That suitcase was to take all my worldly goods on a long flight over the Atlantic followed by an on-going four-day railway journey across the Canadian Prairies.

27 March 1953
On board BOAC Royal Mail Aircraft 'Centaurus'.

Dear Mother and Father
I arrived at the Airways Terminal in Victoria by taxi and found five of my old shower there. I also met a chap from school who had been training in the Isle of Man. As it was raining outside we stayed at the terminal and I rang up Ronald at 4.30 to say that I couldn't see him as we were due to take off at seven o'clock that night. At half past five we took a bus to London Airport (quite a long way) and after waiting about a bit we boarded our BOAC Stratocruiser and eventually took off. It is like a very posh bus except for a bar and small lounge down a flight of steps. There are free cigarettes, cocktails etc. After 90 minutes we landed at Shannon (Ireland) and had supper (free) 4 slices of steak, 4 small spuds, 30 peas etc.
We flew through the night and at

4.15am local time (8.15 English) we arrived at Stephenville, a US station in Newfoundland where we had a cup of coffee in a snack bar. There was a slot machine for Coca-Cola. It was there that we first heard the American accent.

We are now on our first daylight flight from Newfoundland to Montreal. The plane is very steady and one only feels slight vibration from the engines and a very gentle rolling movement. On our way to Ireland it was bumpy, jerking about a bit in the air. We are just passing over the coast of Newfoundland at 10,000 feet — the country seems like a mixture of frozen lakes, snow covered mountains and fir trees. During the Atlantic crossing I went to sleep quite easily in my adjustable seat covered by a blanket. There is plenty of reading matter, magazines, information on the plane etc. I will probably send a postcard with a picture of Centaurus if I can get one. We are going to have breakfast soon on little tables which clip onto the chairs in front of us. Below us at the moment are large quantities of broken up icepacks floating on the sea. I can see land out to the left. The pilot's cabin door is open and I can see him at the controls. I really haven't much more to say at the

moment except that this is an experience
worthy of a full letter card. Nothing like
this has ever happened to me before — a
Tiger Moth seems like a wheelbarrow
compared to this. Breakfast consisted of
orange juice, cornflakes, bacon, egg, sau-
sage, mushrooms, cream, marmalade and
rolls. It was brought by an air hostess.
Love to all from James.

The four-engine propeller-driven Boeing
Stratocruiser, developed from the American
bomber that dropped atomic bombs on
Japan, could cruise one hundred passengers
at a breath-taking (at the time) 340mph, and
BOAC were operating this type on a regular
transatlantic service. When I embarked with
my fellow would-be pilots, nobody told us
that a few months before a door had blown
out of a Stratocruiser's pressurised cabin
causing a passenger to be sucked out never to
be seen again.

I should mention here that two months and
four days before I was due to leave the RAF,
Centaurus was involved in a strange event
that is still being talked about sixty years
later. Perhaps too far-fetched to hit the
headlines, I came across news of it in an
article headed WE WERE SHADOWED
FROM OUTER SPACE in the December

1954 edition of *Everybody's Magazine*, which I still have. Veteran pilot Captain James Howard (until then as sceptical as anyone else about UFO sightings) was at the controls of *Centaurus* on 29 June 1954 on a flight from New York to London. Cruising at 270 mph at 19,000 feet with the sun setting out to his left, Howard saw a dark blob about five miles away, with several smaller blobs clustered around it like bursts of wartime flack. The central blob appeared to continually change shape as it flew parallel to the aircraft for a full 18 minutes while its six smaller attendants switched position around it. This extraordinary sight was witnessed by all eight crew members and fourteen of the 51 passengers, those who hadn't yet retired to their sleeping berths.

After take-off from London our aircraft was scheduled to stop for fuel at Shannon in Northern Ireland and then take the shortest route to Gander in Newfoundland, a distance of just under 2000 miles. In the event we landed ten hours later a few miles west of our expected landfall at Stephenville, a United States Air Force base on the western side of Newfoundland Island. The Yanks were there because of some deal between Churchill and Roosevelt during WW2.

30 March 1953

Dear Mother and Father
After breakfast on the plane we landed as scheduled at Dorval airport Montreal and were herded into two enormous single-deck buses that set out for the city-centre, quite a long way, and our luggage was unloaded at the CPR railway station. The station doors opened as you went through as if by magic. The station was full of Americans and Canadians wearing wide-brimmed hats, light-coloured spacious suits and rimless specs. All the porters were black and wore red pillbox caps. By 10am we were free to amuse ourselves in Montreal. We walked round the city dodging cars, drinking milk shakes and honey dew. We rode back to the station in a tramcar on straw-covered seats and had lunch at the station. I had chicken, oxtail etc (!!) After that we went back to town and I changed all my sterling for dollars, dimes, nickels and quarters. At 3 o'clock we were back at the station to board the train at Track 8. Nearly twelve hours later we got out of the train and were taken to London RCAF Station where we will stay put for the next two weeks. We got to bed by 4am. As half our luggage was left at the

station *I went to sleep in my vest and pants. In the morning we got up and had breakfast — grapefruit, 2 eggs, 2 rashers of bacon, chips etc. We filled in forms and at 9am were given a rather light-hearted introductory talk by our Canadian Flight Commander. In the afternoon we went into London where there is a river Thames. Oxford Street, etc, etc. We saw a three-dimensional film that was quite interesting. In London there are traffic lights with traffic cops who blow whistles to stop the traffic when the lights change! Needless to say they wear guns. Later on we met a chap who came from England nine months ago and joined the RCAF (not as a NATO trainee) he is now a professional magician. We are going to see Niagara Falls on Wednesday and on the 10th we leave here and I'm probably going to start my training in Calgary or another place near there. It means a four day train journey. We will be right near the Rockies and our magician friend told us that they still wear ten gallon hats and spurs out there. The main thing one notices in a camp like this is the terrific central heating in all buildings and very rich food. By the way, when we were in London yesterday we went to the Tudor Café, an imitation of*

English style. The owner is English and is always very good to us types — he knew Darlington quite well and another chap we met went to school in Northallerton.

Love from 2548196 APO James S Stevenson,

NATO Trainee, RCAF London, Ontario, Canada.

Looking back on it now, Canada was like a vision into the future. The cars had flashing lights front and rear to indicate which way they were about to turn, somewhat more reliable than those orange fingers that flipped out of slots on the sides of cars back in England. I'll never forget my first sight of traffic lights telling pedestrians when to cross the road, nor our first admonition by a Canadian policeman: 'Hey, no jaywalking fellers.'

Our introduction to the Royal Canadian Air Force at London Ontario was largely aimed at our French, Italian, Danish and Dutch colleagues who, like the Brits and Canadians, had been enrolled in the NATO Flying Training Scheme. Lectures included a crash course on how the British Commonwealth was ruled over by a monarch (as yet uncrowned) who is not allowed to interfere with the workings of her Democratic

Government. We received dire warnings about the dangers of cold and the scourge of frostbite. Our French Canadian instructor explained: 'When it is cold, do what the Eskimos do — go to bed with the missus.' I closed my eyes and imagined life-saving warmth filtering through my body from an eager bedmate with raw fish on her breath.

The Canadians were very hospitable and seemed extremely keen to introduce us to the wonders of their BIG country. During my first week we were taken on a one-day 200 mile there-and-back trip by bus to Niagara Falls. I'll never forget the sight of that mighty cascade as I paid my toll, took the leaflet and walked across the Rainbow Bridge (202 feet above the water and 950 feet in length) to the United States with thunder in my ears and spray on my face from 600 million gallons per minute plunging over a long curving cliff of rock.

In America I bought a marvellous camera and, from that moment, photographed everywhere and everything and still have a wonderful black-and-white record of those amazing times. Back on the Canadian side I took a walk downriver. On a path close to a vertical-sided gorge I read an inscription on a metal plaque . . .

ON SEPTEMBER 8 1860, BLONDIN, WITH EDWARD PRINCE OF WALES WATCHING, CARRIED HIS MANAGER, HARRY COLCORD, ON HIS BACK OVER THE GORGE DIRECTLY ABOVE THIS SPOT. BLONDIN OFFERED TO TAKE THE PRINCE ACROSS BUT THE PRINCE DECLINED. THE PRINCE OF WALES WAS SO IMPRESSED WITH BLONDIN'S PERFORMANCE THAT IT IS SAID THAT HE PRESENTED HIM WITH A PURSE OF GOLD COINS. BLONDIN WAS THE FIRST TO CROSS THE NIAGARA GORGE ON A ROPE. OVER THE YEARS ELEVEN OTHERS CROSSED THE GORGE BUT BLON-DIN IS NIAGARA'S BEST KNOWN FUNAMBULIST.

Looking over the edge at the foaming Niagara River, 160 feet beneath my toes, made me wonder if vertigo might one day be my downfall, quite literally, a weakness that the Royal Air Force had so far failed to detect.

On 24 March, shortly after our wonderful visit to Niagara Falls, Queen Mary, mother of our late king, died during a peaceful sleep in far-away England. All Canadian and British Air Force personnel based in London Ontario were ordered to attend a hurriedly put together parade. Snow was falling as we marched to a civilian church with surprisingly large crowds of civilian mourners lining the streets.

I was lucky to have the address of a civilian family, friends of my parents who lived in Toronto. As I would very soon be leaving Ontario and travelling west to join a Flying Training School in Alberta, I decided to look them up during my short Easter leave.

Thursday 10 April 1953

Dear Mother and Father
Last Thursday evening our Easter leave started so. I decided to go to Toronto and look up Mr and Mrs Hillier (one of the Bullemore's addresses). Two of us went — Mike Massey and myself. We hitch hiked there, a distance of 125 miles in one hitch in a 1953 Pontiac owned by a commercial traveller. It took about three hours. We got to Toronto about 9.30pm and stayed at the YMCA club of which we are now members. I had phoned the Hilleys a few days back suggesting a visit on Good Friday morning. We phoned again on Good Friday and Mr Hilley said he'd collect us from the YMCA at 12.30. He and Mrs Hilley turned up at the arranged time and place in a very

old Chevrolet (one year old to be exact) and we drove to see Toronto University etc. That evening we had a tremendous dinner of roast lamb, which was quite delicious, and went to the pictures to see a British film all about an American visitor to an old English village. We spent the night at their house and were kept busy enjoying ourselves for the next few days. We were taken to the Granite Club catering for every sport you care to mention, ice-skating, swimming, bowling, curling, dancing etc. On Saturday we went to a dance there with Ruth Page (a niece living with them) and a school friend of hers. Ma and Pa were skating on the ice rink while we were dancing. Later I had a skate on Pa Hilley's skates with two chaps holding me up! On Monday we went to the museum and saw the best Chinese collection in the western world and a horde of other stuff. We were also taken round a big construction job going on in Toronto — a half-built underground railway. One night we watched TV at the Granite Club. Unknown to the Hilleys we ordered a big bowl of flowers (growing in earth) to be sent round after we had gone with a note saying thank you. I shall be travelling 3000 miles by train to Calgary on Friday (10th) where we will start flying *in about a fortnight. I have certainly seen some funny things — in one store the attendants serve you on roller skates because the place is so big. Hilley, by the way, is a lawyer and QC, his wife and he are mad on architecture and some of the work they've done on their large suburban house is amazing. I will be sending you a postcard of Niagara Falls which we visited on 1st April While there I crossed to USA and bought a camera for 29 dollars — very good value — will be sending snaps from time to time. That's all for now.*

Love from steak-a-day Steve.

I later discovered that the Toronto Transit Commission invited Ontario Premier Leslie Frost and Mayor Allan Lamport to open the Yonge Subway on 30 March 1954. Something I purposely didn't mention in my letter home was the softness of Ruth Page's cheek against mine while we danced with her scented hair across my face and tight breasts against my chest. That night I dreamed about Ruth Page. Sometimes I dream about her now.

5

Canadian steam locomotives were not unlike those seen in western movies: very large, very slow with single headlight and with cow-catcher at the front. After a memorable Easter holiday I boarded the train at London Ontario pulled by one of these monsters. We found our allotted seats and, while the train steamed steadily westward, enjoyed a lavish supper in the dining car. When we returned to our compartments the seats had all been converted to sleeping berths for the night.

Tuesday Night 14 April 1953

Dear Mother and Father
We left London (on the river Thames, in the county of Middlesex but nevertheless in Canada) at 7pm on Friday 10th. The train had double-tier bunks which were very comfortable indeed. The beds folded back to make seats in daytime. The following morning we woke up to find we were in a thick forest (birch and fir trees) and emerged into open country with lots of rocks and many small lakes. The last

carriage of the train had an open end from which I got a good view of the scenery — it really was such an unusual sight that I spent quite a lot of time in that end carriage. Here and there we would see a log cabin by the railway line and once I saw a rough looking chap with a gun and two dogs crossing the line behind us, he waved energetically at the train. By the way, everything was covered in snow, lakes frozen but with sun shining, which made everything extremely bright. By about 5.30pm we reached the north shore of Lake Superior and here the railroad (as it is called) ran along a sheer cliff face with the lake several hundred feet below us. At the lake side we saw great piles of logs close to a wood pulp mill.

One fun-loving steward eagerly told us all about the ever-changing scenery that slid past our window. He explained that we were travelling on a single-track line interspersed with the occasional 'passing-loop'. He also told us that our driver knew exactly when our train would arrive at each and every one of these loops — and would know whether or not to take our train into the loop to allow an oncoming train to pass.

I spent hours looking out of the window

considering if perhaps I should have stayed in England and opted for the reserved occupation of farming rather than National Service and the unlikely chance of becoming a fighter pilot. During the 1950's farming was classed as a protected occupation and considered every bit as important as defending the shrinking British Empire. But no, I had set off on a truly amazing teenage adventure, a once-in-a-lifetime journey that I wouldn't have missed for the world.

On the third day we stopped at a small country station called Portage la Prairie, it reminded me of my favourite book, *Farmer's Glory* by Arthur Street, the autobiography of a farmer's son who left his family farm in Wiltshire and shipped out of Liverpool in September 1911 to work on a farm in Alberta. Street got off the train at Portage, was met by his employer and driven in a horse and buggy to a remote farm. He fell in love with Canada in spite of two years back-breaking work at sub-zero winter temperatures. I asked one of the stewards about the name — what did the word Portage mean. He smiled at my ignorance: 'Half the population of this country speak French. Portage means carry — when the river ends you carry your canoe over La Prairie from the Assiniboine River to Lake Manitoba.'

Two hundred miles further on we stopped at Moose Jaw where some of our party got out to join one of the many Royal Canadian Air Force flying schools. Nobody suspected that little over a year later, literally out of the blue, a terrible tragedy would strike Moose Jaw, a tragedy that would be splashed on the pages of newspapers all around the world. More about that later.

After another two hundred miles we stopped at a small station with yet another strange name. Once again our steward had the answer. Medicine Hat is the English translation of a word used by the local Blackfoot tribe, it refers to the eagle tail-feather headdress worn by a certain Indian medicine man who lost his hat at this place during a battle against a rival tribe.

On Sunday morning we awoke to find that a change in scenery was taking place — the forest or 'bush' was turning into prairie and by the time the sleeping car attendant had folded up our bunks the land had become quite flat. At about 10am we reached Winnipeg where all the navigators in our party left the train. The rest of us also stretched our legs on the Winnipeg platform and were given a 'civic welcome' by the Wartime Pilots and Observers

Association with free cigarettes, sweets, coffee, buns, etc, all handed to us by delightful popsies. After a quick stroll around town we re-boarded the train at 11.15 and went on across the flat prairie with plenty of cattle but no trees. At 9.30 on Monday morning we steamed into Calgary and from there went by RCAF bus to the aerodrome. By this time we had completed a modest 3000 miles.

Calgary was covered in snow with enormous icicles hanging from buildings and cars. Some of these icicles hanging from roofs were over five feet long! This, by the way, is freaky as by now we should be having warm Spring weather, but the sun comes out in the afternoon and shines alright (they tell me it's the same sun that's used in England). We hope to be flying after we've been here a fortnight. At the moment we're trying to absorb intensive gen on how to handle the Harvard (Mark 4) before we attempt to actually fly it. We went over to the hangar today to get a good look at the plane — the instrument panel is about the size of a small table and covered with dials, levers, buttons, plugs, switches, sockets, knobs etc. Our course consists of 12 RAF students. 16 RCAF and 19 FAF (French). All discipline, mess organisation etc is controlled by the Senior Course who laid on a party with free booze in the mess to welcome us to Calgary. On 6 July we are expected to be moved to Penhold, about 80 miles north of here, by reputation the last word in luxurious Canadian Air Force camps. The whole station will be moving there as Calgary will soon close down. We hope to get a day off during Stampede fortnight. The Calgary Stampede is a world famous Wild West show. Everyone goes mad for a fortnight and goes around in ten gallon hats and spurs. There are bronco riding competitions, chuck-wagon races and steer roping to mention only a few. Indians turn up and there's quite a show. I was very pleased to get your letter. I hope Simpson and the mice are well installed and I hope Mother's roll of art is appreciated by the right people at the right time! Our airfield is 3700 feet above sea level and the Rocky Mountains are about 80 miles away, easily visible on a clear day, they look much closer than they actually are. When does or did Ronald start on his next course? If he's not at home you might send this letter on to him. Flying here will probably be totally different to Tiger Moths at Digby and all the theoretical stuff we've learned about airfield procedure, *airmanship and navigation might be of some use after all. We will be doing around 180 hours of flying altogether, half of which will be solo. First solo has to be before 25 hours, if not they ask embarrassing questions! Love to all from James. PS These letter cards are too darn small.*

Currie Barracks was the unlikely name of the airfield where we would attempt to learn the art of flying. It was so frustrating — almost as frustrating as dancing cheek to cheek with Ruth Page. We'd flown the Atlantic in a Stratocruiser, crossed the North American continent in a Canadian National Railways steam train to Calgary where we expected to find the ideal climate, clear skies and no fog. To start with, just like Digby, we were grounded. We could see the aeroplanes, climb into them, smell them, dream about them — but the weather was so awful that the prospect of actually flying one of them once again eluded us. We attended Ground School, still getting acclimatised to Canadian eating after a lifetime of rationing back home. The thaw had started, water dripped off snow-covered buildings but everything froze again at night — resulting in those enormous icicles mentioned in my letter. My mother would have painted a picture of them if she had been there — in watercolour, a medium in which she had considerable talent, so much so that our family was waiting for news of her acceptance into the Royal Academy in London — but it was not to be. She did however become a member of the Institute of Watercolour Artists and her pictures were regularly exhibited in London.

21 April 1953

Dear Mother and Father
Thank you for the letter — too bad about the Royal Academy but I expect you're glad to get your pictures back. By last weekend we'd finished our first fortnight in ground school and were due to go on to flights last Monday morning, but Monday was thick fog, bad visibility and low cloud ceilings, too low to fly, so we spent the morning marking in permitted low-flying areas on our maps (boring). I met my instructor and he showed me round the Harvard.
It is now Thursday — still we are grounded. They say it's very rare to be grounded at this time of year. 20 of our course are in C Flight, 10 in C1 and 10 in C2. I'm in C2 and spent this afternoon over at the hangars doing nothing following

a morning spent at Ground School. Tomorrow morning we will be at flights again (hangar) and in the afternoon we will be in GS again. Each flying instructor normally has two chaps from C1 and two from C2. My instructor has one from C2, that's me. I'm reliably informed that he is a new boy and inclined to be nervous, but he seems alright on the ground. I've taken over 30 photos with my new camera since Niagara Falls — the results aren't too bad, I'll send you some when I have a decent collection. I've been doing a bit of square-dancing and some ordinary dancing. We have a dance every month in the mess here, which is good, we ask girls from the local YWCA. Last week they asked us to their dance and it was great fun. Another big party happens when every member of our course has flown solo, students and instructors have a tremendous party — the bar has to really stock up beforehand, quite a crazy set up on the whole. When you complete your first solo flight you're set upon by fellow students and your tie is cut off just below the knot. You have to wear it like that for the rest of the day — unless of course you want to change into a new one and have that cut off too. The tie (once severed) is hung on the crew room wall with your name, initials and date written on it with white paint. Quite a lot of instruction at ground School is done with American training films, a delightful way of learning — we saw one about a pilot who had to parachute into the sea followed by how to climb into a rubber dinghy — catch fish (with government issue fishing line included in the survival kit) — and how to deal with savage natives on desert islands. About a third of the population of Calgary go about in cowboy clothes but that's nothing to what some people wear — velvet jackets are all the rage and that's for sure, so are ties with cowboys etc on them. I saw one in a shop the other day, a tie-shaped colour photograph of a mounted policeman sitting on a horse drinking from a stream — in the background were the Rocky Mountains and a bright blue sky complete with glorious sunset — 'and that's for sure'. I've had one cup of tea since leaving England — I'll come back looking like a coffee bean at this rate. Last night we had a kit inspection. We laid out our kit in a faint semblance of tidiness and our course director seemed overjoyed, he told us how proud he was etc, etc, etc and we were standing, gaping at him in astonishment (in

*England we were never praised). However
we since found out — or came to the
conclusion — that he must have been
totally bottled.*

Love from James.

Queen's Regulations and Air Ministry Instructions decreed that aircrew employed in the Air
Forces of the United Kingdom and Overseas
Dominions must at all times be equipped
with a parachute. To fly a Harvard — or, in
some future dreamland, a Vampire jet — we
needed to wear seat-type parachutes. The standard twenty-eight foot diameter chute must
be carefully folded into a cushion-sized pack
that exactly fits a corresponding recess in the
aircraft's seat. Parachute packs must also be
very tightly attached to the pilot whether he
be long, short, thin or fat in order to avoid
injury in the event of an actual jump. This
requires four straps, one over each shoulder
and two between the legs. Like RAF Digby,
the Parachute Section was run by a happy
collection of chattering girls who took great
delight in getting us to sit on a mock-up
pilot's seat and then tighten our leg straps
until our eyes watered. While doing this they
took some delight in telling us that escaping
from an aircraft with a slack parachute harness could ruin our marriage prospects. All

this was repeated once every month because parachutes need regular repacking and checking. The theory being that sitting on a parachute during several hours of flying can build up static electricity, enough to prevent the canopy from opening.

Ground School was necessary but distinctly unexciting for teenagers itching to get their hands on real aeroplanes. Nearly half a century later, in 2005, at Old Warden aerodrome near Biggleswade, I met my old friend and fellow student Jack Wilkinson at a reunion of Canadian trained pilots. Jack managed to jog my memory about an incident that I'd completely forgotten about. When some time later, I asked him to put something down on paper, he sent me this email on the subject of *opacity* (the opaqueness of clouds).

Hi Jim, the Opacity Incident was when we were still at Calgary. We had a civilian meteorological instructor whose gestures and histrionics were really over the top. As we waited for him to arrive you gave us a very funny impersonation of him. 'Opacity gentlemen, today we are going to talk about opacity'. Unfortunately he arrived at the door and stood looking on for a couple of minutes before somebody indicated his presence to you.

On the first of May 1953, a warm west wind melted the last traces of ice and snow and blew away the depressing blanket of cloud that had hung over us for so long. Tractors pulled fifty yellow Harvards out of hibernation and into the sunshine. Hefty aero-engines banged into life. We were in business.

Piston-engine aeroplanes have large propellers mounted in front of the cockpit to pull them through the air. Because the engine has to be at the front, the logical arrangement for the undercarriage is two large wheels under the wings and a small bogey under the tail, this allows the prop to spin without hitting the ground. When an aircraft of this type is on the ground it points at the sky thus making it impossible for the pilot to see his way forward. Bumping into fences, the commanding officer's dog, airmen, parked aircraft or other obstructions while taxiing was a crime punishable by extra duties, universal shame or even the chop (chucked off the course and sent home).

May Day was the international distress call, so it was rather appropriate that on May Day 1953 Flying Officer MacGregor signed for Harvard Mark 4 Number 20274 to give me my first lesson. I was delighted at the prospect, certainly not nervous but with no idea how difficult it was going to be. If I'd been sent to Rhodesia or stayed in the UK for my training, I would have trodden a much gentler path. The Royal Canadian Air Force, however, expected me to do my stuff in a two-ton Tessie with a forty-two foot wing-span, retractable undercarriage, variable pitch propeller and — as I later found out — a long list of pilot's obituaries to its name. Not for me was the forgiving De Havilland Chipmunk used by other air forces (half the weight of a Harvard, fixed undercarriage, fixed-pitch propeller and just one step up from a Tiger Moth). Many years later I read a wonderful autobiography by a Battle of Britain pilot. In his book *First Light* the author Geoffrey Wellum praises his instructor Eddy Lewis, but is less flattering about the Harvard. I wrote to Geoffrey Wellum who very kindly gave me permission to quote the following passage from his book, written at a time when (like in Canada in the 1950s) the Harvard was used to train pilots from scratch.

I know that the Harvard has a bad name throughout the RAF, having killed several experienced pilots, but this only goes to make the challenge greater. One thing is very obvious: such combinations as Eddy Lewis and the Harvard aeroplane are what the Royal Air Force used to sort out the men from the boys. Only

*total application is good enough and an all-out
effort is essential if one is to make good.*

I walked out onto the tarmac with Flying
Officer MacGregor. 'You do the external
checks, Stevenson, at least you should know
how to do that.' I removed the filler cap on
the port wing and gave it the finger test
— yes, the level was right up to the top. I
walked round the aircraft with MacGregor
breathing down my neck, inspected fabric-
covered elevators for damage, made sure the
tyres showed no cuts or bulges. I checked
the tailplane, rudder, tail wheel, fuel level on
the other wing tank, went round to the front
to check that the propeller wasn't bent and
found no obvious oil drips from the engine.
These are some of the things I'd learned
during those boring hours in the hangar when
we were unable to fly.

MacGregor pointed: 'Haven't you forgotten something?' I had — the pitot head was
covered with what looked like a gigantic
condom attached to a flamboyant red ribbon.
I snatched it off and handed it to the airman
who was waiting to help us start the engine.
MacGregor said, 'If we take off with that
thing still attached you know what will
happen, we won't know our airspeed, we'll
stall on the approach and very likely crash

and burn. Is that how you want to die, Stevenson?' Three months and ten days later I did stall on the approach and oh so nearly crashed and burned.

I strapped on my parachute, put on my leather flying helmet and climbed up into the front cockpit. MacGregor settled into the rear seat and his voice crackled in my headphones. 'Let me know when you're strapped in and we'll go through the starting procedure.'

'Ready sir.'

The attendant airman, standing by the trolley/ac (big batteries and generator on wheels), stepped forward, plugged a thick cable into a socket on the side of the engine and gave us a thumbs-up. 'OK Stevenson, start her up and tell me how you do it.'

'Throttle forward half an inch, mixture control rich, pitch full-fine, ignition off, battery on, work the fuel hand pump, three strokes on the Ki-gass pump, both ignition switches on, energise the starter motor.' I put my right foot onto the starter pedal, pushed down with my toe and listened to the sound of the starter flywheel as it accelerated to a steady whine.

MacGregor said, 'Wait until it's singing soprano — OK, now!'

I pushed hard with my heel. The whine gave way to a grating sound. The propeller jerked through half a turn and a mighty backfire exhaled a puff of smoke and a sheet of flame past my right elbow as five hundred and fifty sleeping horses came suddenly to life, ready to give their power and obey my command.

Although MacGregor was the master and I was merely the apprentice, I had two and a half tons of metal, ninety-two gallons of high octane petrol and two human lives in my hands. I hardly knew what I was doing but somehow remembered to keep my feet firmly on the brake pedals while winding the engine up to full power. With the whole aircraft trembling and my body shaking I heard MacGregor's voice above the din. 'Don't forget to test the magnetos.'

At this point I should explain that the notoriously dangerous Harvard had some redeeming features. Like the human body most of its vital organs were duplicated in case of emergency. I still have two reasonably good ears, two eyes, two arms, two legs, two testicles, two kidneys, and other duplications that help to keep me alive.

With brakes full on, engine roaring and a nine-foot propeller thrashing the air at over two-thousand revolutions per minute, I switched off the left half of the ignition system. The needle barely wavered. I tested the other magneto in the same way. Both were safe. Desperately trying to remember what to do next I throttled back to tick-over, signalled Chocks Away and began to taxi towards the downwind end of Runway Two-Seven.

'Zig-zag, Stevenson, for God's sake. Zig and look to your left. Zag and look to your right. If you look forward you'll see nothing but a spinning propeller pointing at the sky.'

Crackle — crackle, the voice of a watchful man in the Control Tower said, 'Harvard 274 clear for take-off.'

Macgregor said, 'I have control.' Leaving the ground for the first time in this lumbering hunk behind a screaming propeller was sensational in every sense of the word. The facia in front of me vibrated so much that the dials were almost unreadable. We gathered speed along the runway, up came the tail and from my front seat I was finally able to see where I was going. The rumbling stopped and suddenly we were flying with the control column moving in my right hand as MacGregor made a climbing turn. We flew downwind parallel with the runway at a height of one thousand feet and the engine went suddenly silent as Macgregor pulled back the throttle to make a gliding turn towards the spot from where we had taken off six minutes before.

'Keep your left hand on the throttle and your right hand lightly on the stick while I land.' I must have been nervous (perhaps he was) because he yelled, 'I said LIGHTLY, just follow my movements, don't grab everything so tightly that I can't fly the aircraft.'

We came down and down with the propeller wind-milling. Rumbling pops came from the engine. Just when I thought we were going to crash into the tarmac, the stick came right back between my legs, the nose went up and we sank gracefully onto the runway and rolled to a gentle stop. 'You have control Stevenson, taxi round the perimeter track and we'll do it again, and for Christ's don't bump into anything — zig-zag, remember?'

We lumbered back to the take off point with the occasional disapproving grunt in my earphones. Macgregor did it five more times: take off, climb, turn, glide, land. Lining up for the sixth take off he said, 'You have control, Stevenson.'

I turned the aircraft into wind, lined up, pressed the radio button and asked the controller for permission to fly from his runway. Macgregor again: 'Make sure you keep the aircraft straight during take-off, look sideways, keep your eyes on the edge of the runway until you have enough speed to lift the tail to see forward.'

'Yes sir.' It seemed totally wrong to be hurtling forward at sixty knots while unable to see where I was going — but, after reaching seventy on the airspeed dial and lifting the tail of Harvard 2074, I could see that I was going straight — straight for the grass. Strange forces were at work, yes, strange even though I'd learned about something called precession in Ground School.

The axis of rotation has a tendency to turn at a right angle to the direction of an applied force.

In front of me a nine-foot propeller was spinning at 2,250 revolutions per minute, and I was applying considerable force to its axis. Wow, the aircraft swung to the left and we were heading for the edge of the tarmac and the soft grass beyond. MacGregor yelled, 'I have control.' The right rudder pedal shot from under my foot, he corrected the swing and we took off. 'Don't they teach you people anything in Ground School?' Flying Officer McGregor was rattled and he didn't improve during subsequent flights. As the days went on it felt as though I'd become stuck in a kind of stalemate and began to wonder if I would ever get the hang of it. Whenever I tried to take off my instructor would jump on the controls before I'd had a chance to correct the inevitable swing myself.

6

For the first time in my life I wasn't short of money. Our meals were free and with additional Flying Pay (called Risk Pay by the Canadians) I was receiving 100 Canadian dollars per month, more than enough to get shamefully drunk every night in the Mess. In addition to these riches I had ten British pounds per month accumulating in my UK bank account. Within two weeks of our arrival at Currie Barracks and with money to burn, Mike Massey, Jack Wilkinson, Johnny Rose and I pitched in together and went to downtown Calgary for some retail therapy.

Tuesday 19th May 1953

Dear Mother and Father
Thank you very much for the letter to which I have been unfortunately late in replying. The weather up till today has been absolutely wonderful so we have really been making up on our lost flying hours caused by fog two weeks ago. Navigation in this area is really very simple. 80 miles west are the Rockies that run

North–South, also all the roads run either N–S or E–W, never diagonal. The surrounding country is dead flat prairie, very useful in the event of a forced landing. The Harvard aircraft is really like a Humber Super Snipe, a Ford Anglia being like a Tiger Moth. It is of course a bit more complicated and there are a lot of additional things to remember eg. lowering wheels before landing but I mustn't talk shop too much. The other day four of us went down town and bought a 1939 Ford V8 Super Deluxe car, it is enormous and in excellent condition. It has numerous small amenities such as a cigar lighter, radio and cockpit heater. It's in very good condition apart from a small leak in the oil system that is being put right today. On Saturday we drove to Banff and back — a distance of about 200 miles. We drove 50 miles each. The car with third party, fire and theft insurance cost 400 dollars, about one month's pay each. Driving licences were easy to get without a test. Banff is a town in the Rockies surrounded by a National Park. The mountains are really terrific — just enormous snow-capped rocks with fir trees growing out of them to a distance of about half way up. On our way there we came across notices at the side of the road saying such things as 'Beware of big game crossing road' — 'Caution, blasting in progress, do not pass while siren is blowing.' The roads are very poor compared to English roads and many in the suburbs are no better than flattened mud with potholes and large areas of broken-up surface. My Glynn Mills Bank papers came today — it seems fairly straight forward. Yesterday (Monday) was Victoria Day, which is a Canadian holiday. In the evening we hopped into our little motor and drove to see stock-car racing. This is one of Canada's up and coming sports; the cars themselves were once ordinary cars but have now been stripped of all unnecessary metal such as bonnets and mudguards. In front they must have large metal grid bumpers and no windscreens are allowed. These cars race around a quarter mile track. About 15 cars do about 15 laps. You can imagine the chaos on the corners. One of them (a 1934 model I think) turned over three races running and burst a tyre on the fourth. Other cars lost wheels, tore up tyres and generally got smashed up — one chap had steering failure and crashed into a fence just in front of us; two others went through the fence but we couldn't see them very well from where we were sitting. Yes, the Canadians are really quite a crazy shower! Last week we went to a drive-in theatre (theatres are cinemas by the way) and saw a Western film. A drive-in theatre is an open-air affair with an enormous screen in front of which you park your car. Each car is given a little loud speaker which clips onto the window or some such place — quite a novel way of seeing a film don't you think? Everyone in Canada refers to England as the 'Old Country' and most people over the age of 40 seem to have lived in or visited 'the old country' at some time or other. We call it Gods Country (the name Canadians give to their particular part of Canada) and being away from it for a few weeks makes you realise what a wonderful place England really is. Running a car is much cheaper in Canada. Gas (excuse the word but flying instructors and garage mechanics haven't heard of petrol) costs 40 cents a gallon — for that price you can have 2/3 of a haircut or 4 cups of coffee or send 10 inland letters. One more amusing Canadian novelty is a car laundry. Your car goes in one end on a conveyor belt — gets sprayed with water — then about a dozen people set on it with rags (still on the conveyor belt) and polish it up. It comes *out spick and span, much to the delight of the owner — we haven't risked our car in it yet.*

With love from James

Something that I deliberately failed to mention in this letter was a very close shave, or should I say without any exaggeration, a brush with death. The four co-owners of the car were English, and in those days level-crossings in England had substantial gates to prevent cars crossing the line when trains were due. The level crossing close to Currie Barracks had no gate at all, just a notice saying: STOP. I was driving. Our front wheels bumped over the first rail and were about to lift over the second when something made me look to my right. I nearly had a heart attack. The image is with me today, a massive locomotive was bearing down on us. We escaped with inches to spare.

Ethylene was a student nurse with dark hair, a smiling face and totally fascinated by anyone able to tell her all about the Old Country — especially if they had an English accent. In the nurses' hostel where she lived, dances were held at regular intervals and we student pilots were much in demand at these events. Of course we would then ask them back to our dances in the Mess. Ethylene would say, 'That's for sure' and taught me the standard reply: 'That's for darn sure.' While Ethylene was teaching me to square-dance she was amazed to hear that I had never seen, let alone visited, a drive-in cinema. I was equally surprised that she had never seen the sea, probably because she was born a thousand miles from the coast. I liked Ethylene but I don't suppose our relationship would have progressed beyond the occasional back-seat fumble. Everyone smoked. While lighting Ethylene's Philip Morris cigarette with the Ford V8's cigar lighter I told her that I shouldn't be doing it because her name was prominently displayed on placards attached to the safety fence around our gasoline store at Currie Barracks. DANGER — ETHYL-ENE — NO SMOKING WITHIN 100 FEET. Ethylene was, and still is, a colourless highly flammable vapour with a musky smell, highly dangerous and liable to explode without warning — a bit like the human Ethylene. Sixty years later I sometimes wonder where she is now. If I could remember her surname I might be able to track her down on the World Wide Web.

A favourite pastime in the evening was singing. Ted Rousseau was a French Canadian whose favourite song was *Alouette* (about plucking the feathers from various parts of a skylark's anatomy). Rousseau would stand on top of our upright piano, wave his arms in time to the music and lead us into each line of the song while our Danish pianist (one finger missing from his left hand) thumped the keys with force and skill. The French sang a ruder version of the song accompanied by explicit gestures and would often follow it with —

Dans une tour de Londres,
Y avait un prisonnier, y avait un prisonnier.
Y avait un prisonnier la bite au cul, les couilles
pendants.

None of the English speakers had the faintest idea what it meant and when I asked Belvoir he looked at Lubrano who looked at Dessoude, and all three giggled like schoolgirls. *Soixante-neuf* was another phrase that had the same effect on the French — but what's so funny about a number?

After ten flights with Flying Officer Macgregor I had clocked up a total of nine hours and twenty minutes of instruction — and I was going nowhere. To me the Yellow Peril was a dangerous and unpredictable animal that refused to take off in a straight line or fly at a constant speed or altitude, and trying to put it back on the ground in one piece was life-threatening. What little confidence I had at the outset had abandoned me and my instructor, sensing this, was tensing up more and more and taking over his rear cockpit controls at the first sign of a swing on take-off or a bump on landing. I was getting worse. My future on the course was in jeopardy. While walking back to the crew room after a particularly trying seventy minutes my instructor asked me what the problem was. I told him that all I needed was a bit more time to learn how to correct the swing on take-off. He told me in no uncertain terms that given enough time he could teach his grandmother to fly. I was thinking of all the things his grandmother might have taught him if he'd given her the chance when, still walking to the crew room, he gave me a nudge and pointed to a fenced-off area beyond the perimeter. 'What kind of tanks are those, Stevenson?' When I told him I didn't know he said, 'This is a military air force, Stevenson, not a flying club. Those are Churchill tanks, as an Englishman you should know that. At the rate you're going you'll never make it. And remember this, you'll be sent straight back to England if you haven't gone solo by twenty-five hours of dual.' After that episode I felt rather sorry for stuffy old Flying Officer MacGregor, including his long-suffering wife — if he had one.

My elder brother joined the Royal Navy as a cadet aged thirteen. Now Ronald was twenty-one, serving on board a ship. I wrote him a letter that did not mention my inability to fly an aeroplane.

27th May 1953

Dear Ronald
I hope everything is highly satisfactory with you; things are running OK out here. Our programme is 7.45 am–11.30am Ground School, then 12.30–4.30 Flights. Next day it's Flights 7.30–12.00 and Ground School 1.45–4.00. Later on we'll start night flying when this programme will change. We don't reckon to get much in the way of accidents. I have only seen one Harvard in a really unusual attitude — that was when a chap tipped up onto his nose after going off the edge of the runway. No damage was done to the aircraft and the pilot was merely embarrassed. I have done 13 hours now (we were held up at the start due to very low cloud and fog) and now. I'm due for a very big test after two more hours. The Rockies are 80 miles away and are clearly visible to the west of Calgary (they simplify navigation). The other day we went round

to the station hospital for decompression. 8 chaps at a time were put into a gigantic barrel with seats and oxygen masks. We were then subjected to decompression to a simulated altitude of 30,000 feet. There really wasn't very much to it except for violent popping of the ears. We are having a Coronation dance next Saturday in our mess, which should be good fun. Calgary is full of union jacks and decorated for the Coronation but nothing to compare with the Old Country I suppose. The other day we went to see a show put on by 'The Congress of Canadian Daredevils'. It was a display of driving showing things like a new Ford convertible being shot from a cannon then driving away apparently none the worse for it. The main attraction was a stunt man from Hollywood who holds the world record for rolling cars over without smashing them. 14 rolls is his record, which he intended to beat during this show. It was an old car (about 1939) and after driving it round the track once he drove the two left hand wheels up onto a ramp and turned right over and back onto his wheels — then over onto its side. The car made a nice load of scrap for somebody and was unable to carry on with the show with its bonnet ripped off and roof flattened so that its windows were scarcely

101

visible. The engine was still going. Talking of 1930's vintage we have a Ford V8 Super de Luxe with radio, cigar lighter, heater and engine all of which work. The weekend before last we drove to Banff National Park and back (200 miles) without engine failure or major structural damage. In Alberta you are only allowed to cross the road at street corners and then only if traffic lights are in your favour. One does feel ridiculous standing on the kerb when there isn't a car in sight. That is about all the news.

Love from James.

I can't think why I didn't give Ronald a more detailed description of what happens when somebody suffers from lack of oxygen. The medical officer accompanied us in the decompression chamber and we sat next to him on two short benches wearing oxygen masks. As air was pumped out of the steel cylinder in which we sat, hands on a dial mounted on the bulkhead crept steadily round until they indicated a simulated altitude of six miles above the earth. The MO wanted us to witness a scientific experiment and asked for a volunteer. After a short pause Sergeant Lubrano gave a Gallic shrug and held up his hand.

The MO gave him a pencil and a sheet of

paper clipped to a board. 'Thank you Lubrano. I want you to perform a simple task for us. Write your name on the paper and keep on writing it again and again until I tell you to stop. When you get to the bottom of the page, unclip the paper, turn it over and start again. Are you ready? When I give the word, remove your oxygen mask and start.'

Lubrano started to write. The MO said, 'Watch him while he's writing and let me know if you notice anything unusual.'

Within less than a minute I could see Lubrano's lips turning purple but by now I was suffering from the most horrendous bellyache and unable to speak. Lubrano had gone blue and more than that I could see he was in some kind of trouble. He reached the bottom of the page and dropped the pen. When he stooped to pick it up I noticed his fingernails were a dark shade of grey. When his head lolled sideways the MO got off his seat, knelt in front of him and re-attached his oxygen mask. The effect was immediate. Lubrano perked up at once. On the top line of the paper the writing was perfect, further down not so good. Towards the end of the page Lubrano's signature had degenerated into little more than a wavy line. The Frenchman surveyed his work: 'Who wrote this? Is it some kind of joke?' Questioned afterwards he told us he had felt perfectly normal throughout the exercise.

But the MO wasn't finished. He released the vacuum to bring us back to ground level and pointed to a membrane-covered porthole in the gas-tight bulkhead that separated us from an adjacent compartment. 'The pressure on the other side of that bulkhead has been reduced to a simulated altitude of 40,000 feet. When I break the membrane with this hammer we will experience an explosive decompression as the pressure equalises. This will show what to expect if the pressurising system fails in a high-flying jet.' He wielded the hammer. BANG, flash-fog. I farted, belched, my bellyache was suddenly gone but my ears were bursting. We staggered out of the decompression chamber and over a cup of coffee the MO warned: 'When you're flying above 10,000 feet don't forget to check your fingernails.'

The MO also gave us a weekly lesson on Aviation Medicine. A better name for this might have been How Flying Affects the Human Body. He explained that bellyache and lack of oxygen weren't the only things to affect high-flying pilots. 'Think about your ears — never fly if you're suffering from a cold because it blocks the Eustachian Tube.' Somebody said, 'The what?' and he explained. 'We all have two Eustachian Tubes, they connect our ears to our throats. When climbing in an aircraft the outside pressure reduces and the air in your middle ear expands — I'm sure you're all familiar with that popping sound as pressure on both sides of your eardrum equalises even when driving to Banff. No problem so far, but coming down to earth after a long flight can be hell if you're suffering from a cold. Your Eustachian Tube might be clogged, it won't open and the increasing air pressure is not only painful but can cause permanent deafness. When losing altitude pilots can normally open their Eustachian tubes by swallowing, yawning, wiggling the jaw or pinching their noses and blowing but, if you've got a bad cold, none of these tricks will work and you might end up with a burst eardrum after a rapid descent.'

As exams meant ticking multiple-choice boxes it was possible to score high marks without knowing anything. Multiple Choice was NATO's only option as some students had a shaky grasp of English but I hope that none of my French friends are now deaf after strapping themselves into Mirage fighters and diving to attack enemy tanks during France's struggle against Communism in French Indo China.

I had seen television for the first time in my

life at the Granite Club in Toronto (I can't remember the program because I was sitting so close to Ruth Page that I could feel the clip of her left suspender digging into my thigh). The next TV programme I watched is clear in my mind after more than sixty years. On 2 June 1953 a television set was installed in our mess at Currie Barracks and we saw Elizabeth the Second crowned queen of the United Kingdom, Canada, Australia, New Zealand, South Africa, India, Ceylon, Pakistan and a few other places. Although she became queen on the death of her father the coronation took place a year and four months later. Our Canadian friends were as enthusiastic about the whole thing as we were, Danes, Dutch and French also crowded round the flickering screen. We later discovered that, because of the time difference, reels of BBC film had been flown west across the Atlantic to Toronto by a record-breaking English Electric Canberra jet bomber so that the coronation could be shown throughout Canada on the right date and at the correct (local) time.

In many ways, for me, 1950s Canada was a vision into the future. For the first time in my life I saw winking left/right indicators on cars, traffic lights to control pedestrians, slot machines selling cans of soft drink and steam irons, to mention but a few. Local radio stations didn't exist in Britain and I'd never heard advertising on radio or seen it on television. While driving our trusty Ford V8, with aerial extended, it was possible to keep up to date with English soccer scores and, once a week, we listened to News for North America broadcast by the BBC. We also enjoyed listening to advertising jingles put out by various firms based in Calgary. I remember this one, sung to the tune of John Peel.

Now Jenkins Store is the place to go,
Where the quality's high and the price is low,
Your shopping blues are sure to go
If you stop on the trail outside Jenkins.

Calgary Brewery sponsored various radio programmes but was not allowed to plug its main product in a country where the intake of alcohol by civilians was strictly controlled by means of individual liquor licences. The brewery's advertising was therefore aimed at promoting something more innocent.

This programme is brought to you by Calgary
*   Orange,*
The best friend your thirst ever had.

One memorable day (amnesic for some of us) was when this famous and generous company invited all NATO trainees to a wild afternoon of free beer in the most wonderful place you could imagine: a wild-west drinking den with spittoons, sawdust and sassy barmaids, all hidden somewhere near the heart of this enormous brewery and bottling plant.

To me, everything in Canada seemed BIG. The lakes of Alberta were like oceans complete with beaches with the far shore invisible below the horizon. My ears were sometimes battered by summer hailstones. A farmer told me he was insured against hail damage because a single thunderstorm could wipe out an entire year's income by knocking every grain of wheat to the ground. A sudden hailstorm over the airfield would cause frenzied attempts to get all aircraft into the hangars to avoid fabric-covered ailerons and elevators being ripped to shreds. A.G. Street mentions the destructive power of Canadian hail in his book *Farmer's Glory*, but only after seeing those icy pigeon eggs for myself did I understand what he has talking about.

7

I'm quite certain I would have failed to become a pilot if it hadn't been for Flight Lieutenant Moors, our chief flying instructor. He knew what I needed and he had just the man, a newly arrived instructor who had had recently returned from Korea after a tour of combat in a Canadian-built supersonic Sabre jet fighter. No doubt Flying Officer Riggs was looking forward to a bit of peace after tackling Korean and Chinese pilots armed with Nudelman-Suranov cannons firing 550 rounds per minute at him. I suspected that by now the word dangerous had been stamped on my record, but that didn't seem to worry Flying Officer Riggs. For a man of action he seemed quiet, almost shy. He said very little as we walked out to Harvard 20273 for our first flight together. I taxied out to the end of the runway with barely a comment from the back seat, which for me was something new and surprising. After radioing the control tower for permission to take off and having received the expected reply I pushed the throttle to maximum and the aircraft began to accelerate — but as soon as I had enough speed to lift the tail-wheel, the aircraft made its usual and very violent swing to the left. I froze, subconsciously waiting for the guiding hand of my instructor — but none came, just a calm voice in my earphones: 'Let's stay on the runway, eh?' I immediately sensed that this time I was on my own and Riggs wasn't going to help me — no guiding movement on the rudder pedals, no further advice from the back seat. A solid structure, known as the Control Tower, was enlarging in my windscreen and giving me a simple choice — crash and die or fly and live. In a split second I had corrected the swing and made a shaky take-off; wheels up, flaps up, climb away — and still no interference from the back. Landing was something else. Even the unflappable Riggs was forced to take over when I totally misjudged my height over the runway while attempting to adopt the three-point attitude. Riggs said, 'Keep her coming down. Don't be afraid to get down really low. If you lose flying speed twenty feet above the runway you'll crash.' With Riggs behind me my take-offs improved, my confidence was boosted and my dream of becoming a jet pilot was reborn — but why oh why couldn't I land?

With flaps down and undercarriage lowered a Harvard stalls at 55 knots (about 63 mph). To stall is to fall — no more lift from the wings and gravity takes over. To land this type of aircraft correctly a pilot should fall onto the runway from a height of six inches with all three wheels making gentle contact with the runway all at the same time. This is easy to explain but, for me, doing it correctly seemed impossible. Hit the ground too hard and you bounce up with no airspeed only to fall like a stone from a dizzy height maybe dropping a wing in the process — and when a wingtip hits the ground in a shower of sparks the plane cartwheels, fuel tanks rupture and whoosh. Whenever I banged into the ground and bounced up to ten feet or so, the unflappable Riggs would take over with bursts of throttle and swift movements on the controls. I was getting worried. If I wasn't solo by 25 hours I'd be off the course and on my way back to England to serve out my two years doing something far less exciting.

Aerobatics relieved the monotony and, after a successful take off, I'd look forward to the order: 'Climb to 8,000 feet'. Seven minutes later, after reaching this safe height, Riggs would tell me to start a loop by pushing forward on the stick until we were in a near-vertical dive towards the ground. At 180 knots I'd pull gently back on the controls and the sky, underlined by its horizon, would go down like a lift with the ground coming up behind my back — all this with absolutely no sensation of being upside-down. But if you loop the loop too tightly your cheeks start to droop, G-forces drain blood from your optic nerve and everything goes progressively from grey to greyer and then black — but you are not unconscious so you can easily increase the radius of the loop by easing forward on the stick, this reduces the G force and restores your vision. Flick rolls were fun to do but a good slow roll needed the rudder, first one foot and then the other to maintain a steady altitude during the roll.

Going into a spin, in airman-speak, means falling out of the sky trapped inside a whirling lump of metal. During the early days of flying, and right up to the middle of the First World War, pilots didn't know how to recover from what was known in those days as a spiral dive. It was something that crept up unawares to snatch unwary pilots to their death. Thanks to Lieutenant Wilfred Parke of the Royal Navy, we are now able to recover from a spin. On 25 August 1912, barely three years after Louis Bleriot had made his successful flight across the English Channel, Parke was endurance-testing an Avro biplane over Salisbury Plain. Coming in to land after three hours in the air he pulled too hard in a steep turn and was whirled into a left-handed spin. Nobody knew why he decided to break convention by shoving the stick forward instead of back, but that's what he did. He lived and, as a result, so did countless other pilots, once the practice had been officially recognised, in the years that followed.

When falling towards the ground in an uncontrolled spiral the natural instinct of a pilot is to pull back on the control column — but doing that makes things worse. Flying Officer Riggs assured me of this during my first lesson in spin recovery in Mark Four Harvard 20261. We climbed to 8,000 feet on a sunny afternoon. 'We have to burn off 50 gallons of fuel before we can attempt to successfully recover from a spin.' I didn't like the word 'attempt'. Forty minutes after take-off, Riggs shut the throttle, pulled back the stick until we were pointing at the sky and then shoved the left rudder pedal fully forward. The aircraft shuddered, fell and wham we were spiralling towards the ground, spinning out of control. Riggs showed me what to do, speaking to me as he did so. 'Full opposite rudder. Stick progressively forward until the spinning stops. Recover from the resulting dive.' Straight and level again I glanced at the altimeter and noticed that we had lost 4,000 feet in the process.

'Your turn Stevenson, you have control.' Again we climbed to the regulation height for aerobatics. 'Let's try one to the right. Close the throttle, stick back, full rudder, now we're spinning, opposite rudder.'

Opposite? With my whole body pressed to one side and the horizon rising, falling and turning over and over in front of my eyes I couldn't tell which way was opposite, but Riggs could. 'If you don't know which way you're spinning, look at the bottom needle on the turn and bank indicator.'

I enjoyed aerobatics — but what good was that if I couldn't land? Our final aerobatic usually involved putting the aircraft into a spin, spiralling down to lose altitude before joining the circuit for yet another bone-shattering attempt at landing.

Another break from the monotony of circuits and bumps was cross-country navigation. In Canada this was relatively simple compared to England. To the west we had the Rockies, an endless chain of jagged mountains, snow-capped nearly all the year round, beckoning from ninety miles away. Single-engine aircraft, however, were not allowed to fly over the Rocky Mountains. We also knew exactly where the other points of the compass were because rural areas in Alberta and Manitoba were laid out in square-mile sections that formed a regular patchwork of rectangular plots of 640 acres each. If you asked a farmer the size of his farm he'd tell you how many sections he owned. Communicating roads ran around the perimeters of these sections running north-south or east-west so that Canadian pilots were able to tell their direction by merely glancing at the ground. This layout was also helpful when performing aerobatics — line up on one of those straight roads before looping the loop and then see how far off line you were at the finish.

Massive grain elevators at every railway station provided another aid to navigation. Rather conveniently each one bore the name of the local town in huge letters easily visible from the air. In England RAF pilots refer to the practice of following railway lines as Bradshawing (after the famous Victorian railway-guide writer John Bradshaw). In Canada we went Siloing.

Riggs finally abandoned me on 12 June 1953. I must have achieved something that Communist fighter pilots had failed to do — frighten him half to death. I have to confess that by this time I was beginning to frighten myself, not because I was afraid I might be killed (of course not, I was immortal wasn't I?) but believing myself to be immortal

115

did nothing to dispel a different fear. I was now at a crucial phase in my precarious career with a mere five hours of dual instruction remaining before I would have to fly solo or fail the course. This thought kept me awake at night. I was also mindful that a huge amount of tax-payers' money had already been squandered on me, possibly to no avail.

Could Flying Officer Andrews save the day? Unlike Riggs he was chatty. He made cheery comments while saving us both from sudden death while, all the time, my hours were clocking relentlessly to the cut-off point. On 17 June I made a successful take off with C Flight's Chief Instructor Flight Lieutenant Moors in the back seat. It was a mock solo test — the real thing would happen the following day provided I could convince him that I was pilot material during this flight. Moors said nothing to me during the entire flight but I could feel his hands on the controls as we landed.

On the morning of Thursday 18 June 1953 I woke up fully expecting to see *failed* stamped across my record. While waiting to be summoned to Moors's office I was composing my farewell speech: farewell to Moors, MacGregor, Riggs and Andrews; goodbye Johnny, Mike and Jack (you've all gone solo so you can have my share of the car). Goodbye Canada it was nice knowing you, and . . .

'Come in.' Moors looked up from his desk. 'You'll spend the morning doing circuits and bumps with Flying Officer Andrews. If he thinks you're ready to go solo, you and I will fly together after lunch. It will be your last chance, your final assessment.'

It was a very hot day. The sun beat down and my flying career seemed to be evaporating quicker than the sweat from my body. I firmly believe that Andrews was the most patient man I've ever met. In suffocating heat we practised landings again and all the usual things went wrong — too high — too low — bounce like a tennis ball. Andrews was on the controls most of the time because, quite understandably, he didn't want to die.

So this was it, the end of the road. Oh well, at least I'd tried. I'd flown the Atlantic Ocean in a Stratocruiser (as a passenger); I'd seen the archbishop of Canterbury crowning the queen (on television); doors at Montreal railway station had opened for me (as if by magic) and, on one memorable weekend after driving our trusty Ford to a remote farm, I had hired a horse and ridden Western style quoting lines from a film called *Where the River Bends*.

Back in the crew room Moors put his head round the door and wordlessly jerked his head in the direction of the airfield. A silent session of circuits and bumps followed with me making perfect take-offs but, to my dismay, Moors was on the controls every time we landed. After forty minutes his voice crackled in my headphones. 'I've had enough of this. Taxi back to dispersal.' I stopped the aircraft opposite the crew room and Moors took some time unhitching his control column and securing his harness across the empty seat before climbing down. I was about to shut down the engine when I felt a hand on my shoulder. I took off my flying helmet to hear what he was saying.

'You're far too dangerous for me, Stevenson. I have a wife at home who enjoys my company. You're on your own. Do one circuit and land, and if you believe in God say a prayer on the final approach.' He turned abruptly and, as he walked away, I suppressed a yell of joy.

I couldn't believe it. I was aware of the danger but I didn't care. I had climbed over twisted wings in the station scrap yard and seen a pair of abandoned shoes on the floor of a mangled Harvard's cockpit, but I felt elated and marvellous and wonderful. Moors had entrusted me with two tons of Yellow

Peril and the sky above was blue. Very soon I would be up there alone thanks to Macgregor, Riggs, Andrews and Moors.

My First Solo should have lasted no more than fifteen minutes — time enough to take-off, climb to a thousand feet, turn downwind, put my wheels and flaps down, make a gliding turn, approach the runway and land. My take-off was OK. Everything went well, so far so good — should be simple enough to do one landing and walk away, that's all I had to do. But three overshoots later: too high — too slow — too fast — bugger — bump — bang — bounce — I was embarrassed to think that Moors and Andrews were almost certain to be watching from the control tower. Approach again — lose height — three-point attitude — wobble, rumble, brakes, slow down and YES. I had finally made it.

I taxied back, shut down the engine, climbed down onto Terra Firma (the more firmer, the less terror) and was immediately set upon by a group of waiting friends who rugby tackled me to the ground and scissored off my tie immediately below the knot. In the crew room Andrews shook my hand and made quite sure that my severed tie was suitably identified in white paint and hung on the wall alongside all the others. 'You're lucky to be alive, Stevenson. Those approaches were bloody awful and you made a terrible landing, but you did it.' I proudly wore my knot for the rest of the day and celebrated my survival with ridiculous amounts of rye whisky. Thinking about it now I find it hard to believe that we wore ties when flying. The spell was finally broken. From that day onwards my landings improved and my dream to wear the coveted wings of a qualified pilot seemed less remote. I should add that a few days later, my new-found confidence was not helped by a witty ground-crew member in attendance at my third solo: 'Say, you're not taking this thing up by yourself are you? You look younger than my kid brother.' Yes, I suppose I did look a lot younger than my age in those days.

8

Our car had developed some quirky habits. To slow down or stop needed quick thinking and fast reactions not to mention several rapid pumps on the brake pedal but, when the last drop of hydraulic fluid had dripped away, we still had the handbrake. The driver of a car we hit on the way to Banff ignored the dent in his rear wing and helped us locate the hydraulic fluid reservoir hidden under the car floor. We topped up at the next garage. After that we carried a gallon tin of the stuff at all times.

Back on the road to Banff, enlarging mountains dominated the western skyline. Johnny Rose was the only member of the V8 owners' syndicate who had willingly chipped in his quarter share without having the faintest idea how to drive a car. He was, however, the only RAF student on our course who had held a UK private pilot's licence since the age of sixteen. Johnny developed his own unique style of driving. He'd lean his entire body in the direction of the turn when negotiating curves and corners as if banking an aircraft in a turn. Driving our thirteen-year old Ford V8 was a lot of fun but she never failed to remind us of her maturity when climbing the foothills of the not-so distant Rockies during that wonderful summer of 1953. As we climbed, so did the needle on the temperature dial — or altimeter as we christened it.

Banff in the summer was, and probably still is, a truly amazing place to spend a weekend. It's a small resort town with wooden buildings set in the heart of the Rockies surrounded by snow-capped mountains rising to over ten thousand feet with pine forests on all sides. Lake Louise in the middle of Banff National Park provides a magnificent setting for an upmarket hotel called Chateaux Lake Louise — and yes, it looked just like a French chateau or a king's palace in a fairy tale. Slopes above the tree-line, popular with skiers in winter, had a chairlift that operated throughout the year. Suspended high above the forest we took an easy ride to the upper slopes and down again to the shores of the lake where the silence was so intense that we found ourselves talking in whispers. We hired horses, rode the forest trails and promised ourselves to return to this place, which we did on numerous weekends.

Canada taught me the pleasures, but also the evils, of drink. Although only eighteen I was a temporary member of the Royal Canadian Air Force and therefore unaffected by strict drinking laws designed to keep civilians sober, especially those under twenty-one. Our mess had no such limitations and we quaffed Canadian Club rye like veterans while threatening our lungs with un-tipped Export or Philip Morris cigarettes.

We shared the mess with our instructors. On average they were about fifteen years older than us and every one of them appeared to have a limitless capacity for booze. When a group of instructors got together for an evening session it was not unusual to find them drinking Red Eyes at breakfast, attempting to sober up after a heavy night — though how a mixture of beer and tomato juice could be expected to do this I shall never know. What about Queen's Regulations? Didn't these people know that drinking within eight hours of flying was strictly forbidden?

One morning, while walking out to the aircraft, my instructor confessed he was still drunk and would be incapable of helping me if I messed up on landing, although I'm still not certain if this was just a ploy to improve my concentration. Another instructor's trick, within seconds of touchdown, was to unhitch the rear control column and give his student a poke in the back with it. Drunk or sober, there is no way an instructor can take control of an aircraft if he hasn't got a joystick.

Penhold was surrounded by agriculture, and our low-flying area had been carefully sited to cause minimum disturbance to livestock and farmers. Shortly after arrival we were issued with maps of the area on which we circled these few and far-between low-flying areas. On 6 July I took my instructor Andrews on a familiarisation flight over the surrounding country — I say 'took' because by now I had miraculously managed to take-off and land without him jumping on the controls to save himself (and me I suppose) from death. In due course we went low-flying in one of the designated areas, and this time I say 'we' because low-flying was strictly against the rules for solo students. While dodging tree-tops and telephone wires and zooming over flocks of dust-raising turkeys, Andrews told me about the low-flying book. 'If you ever need to low-fly outside the area, don't forget to sign the book as soon as you get down. Don't laugh, it can happen — low cloud, loss of power.'

Aeroplanes are speed-friendly and SLOW means DANGER — they only fly because air whizzes over and under the wings to keep them up. STOP and you DROP. Speed is good and it's also exciting. I was glad when Andrews said, 'Take me to the low-flying area.' Hurtling at grass-top height at some ridiculous speed with Andrews in control, we had to climb to clear a line trees. 'You have control, Stevenson.' Just as I was levelling off at 2000 feet, the throttle jumped backwards out of my hand and the engine seemed to stop, or at least quietened to a series of pop-pop-pops behind a wind-milling prop. 'Simulated power failure, Stevenson. Pick a field.' It wasn't a difficult choice. A huge grassy field lay immediately below. 'Your engine has failed. We are now gliding. Circle the field and make your approach into wind.' How was I supposed to know where the wind was coming from? 'Bonfire smoke, Stevenson, over to your right, can you see it? Now remember this, when force-landing never lower your wheels.'

I needed no further explanation because I already knew the reason for that. We glided down with the engine backfiring. 'Watch your airspeed. Keep coming down.' I was sweating. Blades of grass made a green blur under the wing. Just as I really believed that Andrews was expecting me to actually belly-flop onto the field, he said, 'I have control.' Thank God, I thought. Walking away from two tons of dead aluminium crashed in a field with fractured tanks containing enough fuel to propel the average family car for a thousand miles was something to be avoided, even for a teenager who believed himself immortal.

Flying back to base I thought about my father's cousin Margie Fairweather, one of the 166 female pilots of the Air Transport Auxiliary who delivered aircraft from factories to RAF squadrons during WW2. In the spring of 1944 Margie was flying with two passengers in a fixed-undercarriage Percival Proctor. She suffered engine failure and attempted to put down in a farmer's field. Unfortunately the wheels dug into a hidden rut and the aircraft flipped over. Margie's passengers survived but she was killed. If she had been flying a Harvard she would have been able to land wheels-up and survive.

All four owners of a certain Ford V8 Super-Deluxe were beginning to worry about a disturbing sound coming from deep inside the engine of our Ford V8. A once muted tap-tap-tap had gradually increased to a staccato BANG-BANG-BANG that turned heads wherever we went. Scrap it or repair it — something had to be done double quick. At the bar we were discussing options when Flying Officer Waddell joined us. 'Use your brains,' he said, 'tackle the problem. You've been bored to tears in Ground School learning about the mysteries of the internal combustion engine — now's your chance to get your hands dirty.' By the time Waddell had told us what was on his mind he was already on his fourth rye-and-ginger (paid for by us). I passed round my packet of cigarettes as he continued: 'One of your eight big-end bearings has failed, the piston is hammering the cylinder head, but it's not the end of the world. Nothing to it, piece of cake.'

We believed him. Nobody was better qualified than Wadell, who'd still be working in a Ford car factory if he hadn't dusted off his uniform and rejoined the RCAF to teach us how to fly. 'Undo the securing bolts, lift the front of the engine by two inches, undo the nuts attaching the sump and it will drop down nice and easy. All V8 production from 1937 onwards have replaceable big-end shells so you can do the job yourselves at low cost, apart from the drinks each one of you is about to buy me.' While drinking his umpteenth rye he asked the steward to find the local newspaper. He glanced quickly through and pointed to an advert. 'Take a look at this.'

Mend cars at FIX-UR-SELF with speed,
We have all the tools you need.
FIX-UR-SELF has hoists and pits

Spare parts and all the bits.
We give advice, so don't waste cash.
Fix your auto in a flash.
We are open all week through,
And don't forget — on Sundays too!

Always ready for a challenge the four of us took an ignominious tow into Calgary one Saturday morning determined to complete the job and drive back to camp by Sunday night. We found the garage. Every facility was ready for us: hoists, tools, spanners and spares. Following Waddell's instructions, we removed one of the cylinder heads and located the offending piston, which had a shiny ring around the top where it had been clouting the cylinder head. Remembering what we'd been told we undid the forward bolts and hoisted the front of the engine by two inches using chains and pulleys. Together we undid all the bolts around the sump but it would only drop a few inches at the forward end leaving just enough space for me to insert my arm. Working blind I located the offending big-end bearing, extracted both split pins with a pair of pliers, unscrewed two castellated nuts and withdrew the lower half of the bearing complete with its chewed-up shell. No wonder the engine had kicked up such a racket. After replacing the shell and still working in the dark, I tightened the two nuts but was unable to replace the split pins. With the engine running would the nuts work loose? Probably, but it was a risk we had to take. The engine started first time and we drove back to base with fingers crossed and the engine purring like a kitten.

9

Aeroplanes are dangerous, so are cars. Students and instructors crashed their cars so often that our Commanding Officer summoned all personnel to a vigorous pep-talk in the camp cinema. 'I don't know what goes on in France, Britain, Holland, Denmark or Italy, but here in Canada the curves on our roads are engineered for speeds no greater than forty miles per hour.' This solemn warning reminded me of a popular song on a 78 record that we played so often its Bakelite grooves were almost smooth. The introduction to the song was a deafening squeal of brakes followed by crunching metal.

> *That crash you heard a minute ago was me falling for you.*
> *It wasn't a tramp tripping over the trash,*
> *It wasn't a Ford running into a Nash,*
> *That crash you heard a minute ago was me falling for you.*

But it wasn't a badly engineered curve that, once again, nearly killed all four Ford V8 owners. Massey was the culprit, a chap who seemed to lose all sense of self-preservation when sitting behind the wheel of a car. Driving 'off-piste' on a mountainous track he led us into an ever-narrowing muddy path with a wall of rock on one side and a sheer drop into a ravine on the other. I was sitting in the front next to Massey when the unlevel track made the car slide sideways towards the ravine. I was terrified. I tried to avoid looking down into the chasm but when the car took another sideways slide I'm ashamed to say I made matters worse by instinctively grabbing the steering wheel, the only solid thing within my reach. Massey seemed totally unaware of the danger — and our back-seat passengers never said a word, frozen with fear as they later admitted.

We had barely completed two months flying when No. 4FTS moved to another airfield about eighty miles away. On 2 July 1953 a mass formation consisting of 44 Harvards flew from Currie Barracks to Penhold. A local newspaper described it as the most dramatic sight ever seen in Albertan skies. My instructor wanted me to fly with him, which I did, leaving Wilkinson, Rose and Massey to make their own way in the Super De-Luxe. The aircraft left Currie barracks in an ear-splitting aerial traffic jam of yellow metal with the tips of all those nine-foot propellers breaking the sound barrier.

Penhold was the latest, the most amazing wonder and proud boast of the Royal Canadian Air Force with large dormitories, comfortable beds, chromium-plated bar, snooker and ping-pong tables. Exhorted at all times to keep ourselves smart and tidy we used a high-tech twin-tub machine to wash our clothes and wonder of wonders, we also had the latest achievement in domestic science — an electric iron with built-in water reservoir that puffed steam onto your trousers at the press of a button.

Indoors everything was hunky-dory but viewed from the outside the whole place seemed to be sinking into a sea of mud. The only way from sleeping quarters, to mess hall, to class-rooms or to flights required a balancing act along half-submerged duckboards.

One evening I drove our Ford V8 to the oil boom-town of Red Deer, ten miles away, with co-owners Massey, Rose and Wilkinson together with a sergeant in the French Air Force. We were heading for a dance hall because Johnny Rose had persuaded us all that it was high time we had a go at square dancing. We stopped in a crowded car park and heard music as soon as we got out of the car. Dancing was in full swing with an old-timer fiddling away on a violin pressed against his ribs and a caller shouting above the din: 'Circle left and circle right — hold that gal, oh so tight — forward and back, lead her through — lift your heels for a dosado.' The place was heaving and before we had been there three minutes our Frenchman grabbed a redhead and was obeying orders by holding her oh so tight in a throng of whirling dancers. Not to be outdone we Brits danced but failed to grab, only pausing to replace sweated-out fluids at the bar. At the end of a wonderful evening the five of us piled into the trusty Ford and headed back to Penhold. Before we'd travelled half a mile our Gallic friend said he wanted go back to the dance hall, trying to convince us he'd made an arrangement to practise soixante-neuf with la belle rouse. Mike Massey, who was driving, ignored these pleas, insisted we all go home to bed and put his foot on the gas — whereupon the Frenchman opened the rear door and jumped. He was absent at breakfast the following morning but when I met him in the crew room he showed me a badly grazed elbow.

Summer was coming so we Brits changed into our khaki drill uniforms. Towards the middle of June 1953 we started seeing advertisements in the Calgary Herald, a newspaper distributed throughout Alberta.

The Calgary Stampede Opens Monday July 6 at 9am: monster street parade, commercial floats, bands, Indians, pioneers. See the world famous chuck wagon races. A thrill every second. Brahma bull and steer riding — rough, tough and dangerous. Championship saddle and bareback bucking horse riding. Calf roping, wild horse races, wild cow milking. Livestock show, stage shows, vaudeville, music and dancers, fireworks and farm machinery. Accommodation plentiful.

This we had to see. Jack Wilkinson, Johnny Rose, Mike Massey and Steve (as I was known in those days) donned our civilian clothes and piled into our newly-repaired Super De Luxe. When we got to Calgary the streets were jammed with parades of baton-twirling girls, men on horses, elaborate floats and cheering crowds. Feeling underdressed we bought wide-brimmed Stetsons at the first opportunity. I still have mine, the leather sweat band is in tatters but it keeps the sun off my face while gardening and my grandchildren tell me it's 'cool'. Suitably attired we bought tickets and walked past a hoarding inviting us to see Canada's finest livestock.

We saw nearly everything described on the poster but when a dozen unbroken mustangs bolted into the ring the scene that followed was something to remember — cowboys lassoing horses, mounting them bareback and falling into clouds of dust so thick that we could barely see what was happening. The wild cow milking contest sent buckets flying in all directions with contestants darting through the chaos trying to be the first to deliver the required pint of milk to a panel of solemn judges seated behind a table.

Jack and I were later drawn to a long line of sideshows where a man waved his cigar at us. 'Hiya boys, want to earn some easy cash? If I can't guess your weight within two pounds you win five bucks.' I gave one whole Canadian dollar to the showman who looked me up and down as if judging a cow. He squeezed my forearm, turned me round, put his arms around my waist, patted my buttocks and wrote 147 pounds on the back of my ticket. I felt mildly self-conscious sitting on a metal chair suspended from a large dial but incredibly he had judged my weight within two pounds. I lost my dollar.

We wandered on and very soon an exciting neon-lit invitation shining above a half-open door attracted our attention. We paid, entered a gloomy tent and sat on folding chairs in front of a dimly lit stage. After a long wait, during which nearly all seats were filled, the curtains opened to reveal a muscular lady who fluttered her eyelashes and dropped her dress in a series of ungainly swivels, bumps and grinds. She fumbled behind her back in a drawn-out attempt to unhook her brassiere while raucous voices shouted encouragement: 'Take it off.' Fumble, fumble, 'Take it off, take it off.' Off came the bra and in one disappointing moment it became clear that 'she' was a he. I nudged Jack and we made for the door. We drank several beers that afternoon. 59 years later I couldn't remember where we spent that night, but when I met Jack Wilkinson at a reunion he reminded me. The four of us drove to our old barracks in Calgary hoping to find accommodation and ended up in the guard room where the Service Police kindly allowed each of us a cell for the night.

Sylvan Lake was our favourite weekend haunt. Drive there in the Ford, hire a boat and fishing tackle, drift peacefully and hope to catch a pike or a perch. On one lucky day we landed a three-pound rainbow trout, made a fire, roasted it on glowing embers and ate it with our fingers. Sylvan Lake, seen from the air, was a glistening rectangle eight miles long and two miles wide surrounded by a thick pine forest. Fishing was fun at weekends, but so was flying low over the water on weekdays in search of a man in a boat, so low that he would be unable to read the aircraft's identification number.

One shiny Canadian Monday, 13 July 1953 to be precise, I headed for Sylvan Lake in Harvard 20310 to practise my solo lesson plan for the day: medium turns, climbing turns, steep turns and spins. I was half way through my climb to 8,000 feet, a height that would leave plenty of sky and time between me and the earth to correct mistakes, when a flash of reflected sunlight caught my eye. A second look identified a Yellow Peril, just like mine, about half a mile away. The sight of it reminded me of a vivid scene witnessed as a child. Here was a Focke-Wulf 190 of the Luftwaffe and something had to be done about it. I was the man on the spot. It was up to me to attack the enemy with my forward-pointing, non-existent machine guns, watch it burst into flames and spiral into the lake. I closed the gap and got close enough to see that my intended victim was flying solo — clearly there was no instructor in the back seat. My Spitfire was closing in for the kill. He was in my sights. I was about to kill him in a hail of bullets — and he reacted exactly as I hoped he would by turning away from me.

He had taken my bait. The fight was on. I opened the throttle as far as it would go and made a steep turn. He kept turning. We flew in ever decreasing circles at full power with me trying vainly to align my 'guns' on the back of his leather helmet. We turned tighter and tighter and I knew that my trout would stay hooked if only I could keep on his tail. My right wing pointed at the lake 4,000 feet below. My left wing pointed at the sky. I pulled tighter and tighter in the turn until suddenly, without warning, my aircraft flicked into a spin.

The long finger of Sylvan Lake twisted towards me, enlarging, whirling round and round, dipping and lifting with my glimpsed altimeter unwinding as the lake rushed up. A voice in my head was saying: shut the throttle, full opposite rudder, stick progressively forward. But the spiral tightened, the spin continued. The lake was like a whirlpool sucking me in. Suddenly the whirlpool froze. The spinning stopped. I pulled out of the ensuing dive and saw the upturned face of a man in a boat. Waves of relief and guilt swept over me as I headed back to base. I had sinned. I had broken the sacred rule — NO DOGFIGHTING. After landing I was able to truthfully tell my instructor that I had completed all the exercises on my kneepad, including several steep turns and a spin.

Shortly after arriving at Penhold, Flying

Officer Ayres taught me how to make a Precautionary Landing, which means approaching the airfield below stalling speed. Paradoxically it's done with the engine running at full power with the nose up so that the propeller provides some of the lift. Ayres explained: 'One day you may be forced to put down on a very short runway and today I'll show you how it's done. You can have a go by yourself when I think you've got the hang of it.'

With all modestly I have to say I took to precautionary landings like a duck to water. It was sheer fun, low-flying over adjoining pastures with my nose in the air before crossing the fence, chopping the throttle and dropping onto the runway like a helicopter and then applying brakes — but not too fiercely because a cartoon on the crew room wall, showing an upended Harvard, was captioned: the Harvard has good brakes — misuse of them will put you on your nose.

Flying 'on instruments' was another skill to be learnt. My instructor explained. 'No pilot has ever been able to fly in cloud without instruments, and by instruments I mean the altimeter, the airspeed indicator and the turn and bank indicator, not to mention the good old artificial horizon. That's why birds stay grounded in fog — no instruments, they can't see which way up they are or where they're going — and neither can you.' I found this difficult to believe — surely you can FEEL if you're upside down and feel if you are turning or diving. No, I was told, 'That's called flying by the seat of your pants, it doesn't work, never try to do it.'

Harvards were fitted with canvas hoods, like the soft top of a sports car, that could be raised inside the front cockpit to prevent the student from seeing what was going on around him (as if in fog) thus forcing him to look at the instruments. At first I found it impossible. When my pants told me I was in a steep turn to the right, the instruments indicated that I wasn't. On one occasion my pants tried to convince me I was flying straight and level when the altimeter was unwinding and the turn-bank indicator showed a sharp turn to the left. Could I really be in a spiral dive? It certainly didn't feel like it.

In Ground School we learned how to survive after parachuting or crash landing in the Canadian wilderness (more of that later). We learned navigation, engineering, how and when clouds form and vainly tried to increase our speed at sending and receiving Morse Code by buzzer or Aldis lamp, amongst many other subjects.

One day Ayres sent me off on a solo flight to practise aerobatics. He said, 'Try a precautionary landing when you get back.' After an hour of loops and rolls I decided that my precautionary landing would include the slowest and lowest approach that Penhold had ever seen. Over farmland, some two miles from the airfield boundary, I dropped to barn-top height, put down full flap and undercarriage, pointed at the sky and gave that nine-foot propeller every ounce of power that Pratt and Whitney's nine cylinders could provide. It felt good. I was in a helicopter with the engine roaring and treetops level with my wingtips. I cleared our boundary, chopped the power, bumped onto the lip of the runway, slammed on brakes and came quickly to a halt. I felt good. Surely this must be the shortest landing that the Royal Canadian Air Force had ever seen. Downstairs in the control tower I was about to sign off the aircraft when I noticed a rather peculiar smile on the duty sergeant's face. 'The air-traffic officer wants you to sign the low-flying book.' Puzzled at this, I asked for the book, opened it and started writing immediately below the previous entry: registration number, reason for low flying, etc, etc. I was still writing when the sergeant told me to stop. Evidently he was in on some kind of joke against me because he couldn't stop laughing. Okay, I'd been well and truly had for a fool but I'd already soiled the pages of the hallowed LOW FLYING BOOK. 'For God's sake give me a rubber.'

'Sure, what size? Or do you mean an eraser?'

I grabbed the rubber and made rather a bad job of removing my entry. That evening I was summoned to the Station Commander's office. Unsmiling officers, including my instructor, were seated around a table. The CO began: 'Ah, Stevenson, would it surprise you to know that we've received a report that your aircraft was seen low-flying in a prohibited area?'

'Yes sir, it would.'

'You made an entry in the low-flying book and then you attempted to erase it — why?'

I explained what had happened and all was resolved.

★   ★   ★

Aeroplanes are heavy. The sight of a Jumbo jet hopping from the tarmac and lifting into the sky after lumbering along a Heathrow runway never fails to amaze me even though experts in aerodynamics have attempted to teach me what makes it happen. Air flows over the wings at a critical speed and the miracle occurs. Speed is crucial for this. One mile per hour too slow and the Jumbo won't lift, it stays on the ground and crashes into the perimeter fence. If attempting to fly too slowly once airborne, the plane drops and hundreds of disappointed passengers find themselves engulfed in flames and tangled aluminium. Stall rhymes with fall. Deliberately stalling the aircraft and letting it fall was an important part of our training: throttle back — lift the nose — reduce airspeed — shudder — judder — and oops there she goes. The Harvard had a wicked habit of tipping over to one side and if left to its own devices would go into a spin. So here's the dilemma: to land an aeroplane the pilot must stall it a few inches from the ground to get that satisfying squeak and rumble from the tyres.

On the morning of 10 August 1953 I was due for a navigation trip with a difference. In the crew room Flying Officer Blaney explained. 'How would you like to break today's navigation flight with a nice plate of eggs-over-easy in the coffee shop at Calgary Municipal Airport?' This was something I'd been waiting for. All students had to do it as part of their training — first with an instructor, then solo next day. 'You work out the flight plan, Stevenson, while I sign for the aircraft.' I plotted the course and estimated our time of arrival at Calgary with due allowance for wind direction and speed. Forty minutes there, forty minutes in the coffee shop, thirty-five minutes to fly home again with the wind in our favour.

'You have control.' I took off without incident and after cruising south for half an hour I could see a lot of activity at Calgary's busy airport. Blaney had already told me what to say so I thumbed the button on the top of my control column and said rather nervously, 'This is Canadian Air Force 141. Request permission to land.'

The answer was immediate. 'Welcome to Calgary, Air Force 141. We are using runway zero-eight-nine. You are cleared to join the circuit.' While watching a Norseman making a gliding turn towards the runway Blaney chose that moment to remind me: 'You have control.'

I pressed the button again. 'This is Air Force 141, request permission to land.'

'Come on in.'

I lowered the undercarriage and made my gliding turn while saying the checks out loud as Blaney had taught me: Pitch full fine. Harness tight and locked. Mixture rich. Undercarriage down and locked with green lights on. As usual Blaney kept his mouth shut as I made what I thought was a carefully judged gliding descent towards a very wide concrete runway that glared white in the sunshine. Conscious of an audience of civilians, I was determined to make a copy-book landing in such a public place. Lower, lower — at three feet above the ground (or so I thought) I rounded out for the perfect three-pointer, the falling-feather touchdown that all pilots strive for but . . . instead of a rubbery squeak a yell came from the back seat: 'I HAVE CONTROL.' The throttle shot out of my hand, the engine roared and Blaney did what I should have done, break the fall with power and sink onto Calgary's concrete with a gentle bump and a comforting rumble. 'Good God, Stevenson, you were ten feet too high on the final approach. We all make mistakes but if you drop below stalling speed when you're ten feet up I don't have to tell you what will happen.' I knew what would have happened if Blaney hadn't taken over: we would have stalled, the wing would have dropped, hit the concrete and the whole kaboosh would have burst into flames. At least he let me taxi to the parking area, which was rather good of him under the circumstances. A man in overalls beckoned to us and pointed to a line of light aircraft. After shutting down I undid my straps and climbed out. Blaney seemed unruffled. 'Fried eggs and a shot of rye in our coffee, here we come.' He made no further comment about our near-death experience.

After the coffee shop we got back into the Harvard. I started the engine and radioed for permission to taxi. Waiting our turn to take off we watched a four-engine North Star climbing away with its heavy load of passengers, once it was clear we taxied out to take our turn. Thinking about it now reminds me how uneasy I felt in spite of that second cup of alcoholic coffee. I knew what lay in store. Tomorrow I'd be doing it on my own — and Blaney didn't seem the least concerned. I hadn't landed at Calgary — HE had landed at Calgary after I had made a complete mess of it in spite of the fact that by now I had 53 hours dual instruction and 20 hours solo under my belt.

The following day I was allotted the same aircraft for my solo flight. I took off in good old Harvard Mark Two number 141, climbed into a clear sky, arrived at Calgary and nervously radioed, 'This is Canadian Air Force 141 — Request permission to land.'

'Roger 141. You are cleared to land on runway 27.'

Glaring concrete again. I glided lower and lower with speed dropping off and no Blaney to guide me. When I judged my height to be no more than two feet off the ground I adopted the three-point attitude and waited for the gentle bump — which didn't come, and didn't come, and didn't . . . the right wing dropped suddenly and in a split second I remembered what Blaney had said to me 24 hours ago. You're ten feet too high. I shoved open the throttle, the giant Wasp engine responded and powered me away in a roar that almost drowned the querulous voice in my earphones: 'Air Force 141, do you intend to land?'

What a question. Yes, I told him, and instinctively made a climbing turn to port to re-join Calgary's circuit on the downwind leg. I was shaking and sweating, trying to visualise the civilian controller who by now would be shaking his head in despair. As I settled into my second approach the question came again. 'Air Force 141 do you intend to land?' Intend to land! Damn the man, of course I did — but then realised that, obviously unused to the antics of trainee pilots, he was asking a perfectly reasonable question. Again I assured him that I intended to land while trying to work out why, just like yesterday, I had made such a massive error of judgement. I came in again, lower and lower: speed 80 knots, flaps down — round out to land . . . Hell's teeth, exactly the same thing happened, miles too high, the wing dropped again but I managed to shove the throttle forward just in time to avoid the crash. Did I say shove? Not a clever thing to do because the pilot's handbook clearly states that a Wasp engine can fail to pick up if the throttle is opened too quickly. It was a hot day but that wasn't the only reason why sweat was running into my eyes.

'Do you intend to land?' The question came yet again but this time I detected a note of irritation. I did intend, and I also intended to eat eggs over-easy and drink coffee with cream and two sugars with a slug of rye. How could I face Blaney with the limp confession that I'd failed to do what every student was expected to do without incident or mishap. With red mist clouding my vision I came in for a third attempt and heard the nagging question for the fourth time: 'Air Force 141 do you intend to land?'

I hesitated before replying. 'No, I'll just touch and go' — and I could hear a sigh of relief in my earphones. Heading for home and feeling wetter than my shirt I asked myself why I had failed to even touch, let alone land, on Calgary's concrete. I felt thoroughly demoralised, wondering if I had somehow forgotten everything I'd been taught. Was I doomed to sail on like an airborne Flying Dutchman until I ran out of juice? Had I suddenly lost all the skills acquired during my hours of flying in the Royal Canadian Air Force? These questions were repeating over and over again as I joined the Penhold circuit where, I'm happy to say, I achieved a text book landing. When Flying Officer Blaney asked me if I had enjoyed my cup of municipal coffee I looked him in the eye and confessed my sins. Instead of tearing me off a strip he laughed, which made me hope that he wasn't going to take it any further. I never knew the reason why I had misjudged my height at Calgary, but 63 years later when discussing the incident with a retired Group Captain I was told that it was fairly common for trainee pilots to subconsciously judge their height by noting where the edge of the runway came in relation to the wings — thus an unfamiliar airfield with an extra wide runway might convince the pilot that he was much lower than he really was.

10

The great day I had been waiting for came exactly one year and twelve days after I'd joined the Royal Air Force. By this time I had clocked up over sixty hours dual instruction and thirty hours solo. 29 August 1953 marked the start of two glorious weeks of do-what-you-want and go-where you-please LEAVE — but for chrisake get your arses back to Penhold by 12 September.

Dear Mother and Father
I don't think I ever gave you an account of our mid-term leave. We started off on a Friday afternoon with Viarouge, a Frenchman, Al Nichol, a Canadian who owned the car, and two Englishmen, John Rose and me. Before leaving we lost valuable minutes extracting Als car from Penholds mud with the help of a mobile cement mixer and then headed south. Two hours later we arrived in Calgary just as it was getting dark where the four of us had a meal in a coffee shop (café). We left Viarouge in Calgary and by 9pm had completed the 167 miles to Number 3

Flying Training School Claresholm where (wonder of wonders) we managed to find three unoccupied beds. Our evening at Claresholm was interesting — we arrived during an APO's party to celebrate the return of the Ashes.

I didn't dare tell my mother everything that happened at Claresholm during that one-night stay. England had just beaten the Aussies at cricket and all the English cadets at Claresholm were in a state of ecstatic frenzy about their country reclaiming a scruffy little urn full of wood ash. I suspect that some of my readers won't have the faintest idea what all this Ashes business is about and I confess that, at the time, I didn't know what started such a quaint legend. Today, however, I can explain. During the reign of Queen Victoria the Sporting Times newspaper lamented Australia's defeat of England by printing the following obituary: 'In Affectionate Remembrance of English cricket, which died at the Oval on 29th August 1882 . . . The body will be cremated and the ashes taken back to Australia.' A short time later a group of Australian women rubbed more salt into the wound by presenting England's cricket captain with a tiny urn containing the ashes of a bail taken from the losing wicket. This must have ruffled a few feathers because ever since those times, England and Australia have fought for ownership of the Ashes in a series of five cricket matches held every other year in alternate hemispheres. Our arrival at Claresholm in August 1953 coincided with the return of The Ashes to England after nineteen years of failure and frustration. A group of English chinless wonders had organised a party to celebrate the event to which we were invited. Without thinking we accepted — and what followed was an eye-opener. It seems that we had stumbled on the remotest outpost of the Royal Canadian Air Force, abandoned by civilisation and populated by students who created their own bizarre forms of entertainment.

After dinner Al Nichol, Johnny Rose and I were propelled into a large room with chairs three or four ranks deep arranged in a circle. A floppy-haired youth announced the first song and led us into the first chorus.

O come and see the Wild West Show.
The elephant and the kangaroo-oo-oo,
We all sing together in all kinds of weather,
Come and see the Wild West Show.

After a very short silence a name was called and people started chanting again and again,

'Sing, sing or show us your ring.' The victim chose to recite as follows.

Ladies and gentlemen, here we have the
   CROCODILE.
'The what sir?'
The crocodile is the tightest-skinned animal in
   the world,
When it winks it wanks.
Stop throwing sand in its eyes sonny.'

The chorus, as before, was deafening . . .

O come and see the Wild West Show.
The elephant and the kangaroo-oo-oo.
We all sing together in all kinds of weather.
Come and see the Wild West Show.

Another name was called. The poor chap stood up but hesitated, seemingly unwilling to make a fool of himself in front of the mob. Everyone screamed at him: 'Sing, sing or show us your ring.'

Without hesitation the youth walked calmly to the centre of the (dare I say it, ring) lowered his trousers and showed us what not everybody wanted to see. Before the applause had died, a small cadet with red hair volunteered the next verse.

Here we have the rhino-sore-arse.
The rhinoceros is the richest animal in the
  jungle.
Sore arse meaning piles, rhino meaning riches.
Hence piles of riches.

Chinless wonders fell about laughing but there was more to come. After an endless repertoire of rude songs the chief bully announced a drinking competition. Johnny, Al and I looked at our shoes while the bully called out a name. The chosen one stood up, apparently quite keen to accept the challenge: 'Do you agree to drink my cocktail?'

Everyone chanted and jeered. The chosen one seemed eager enough until a half-pint glass of green fluid was produced. The victim bravely drank it all down but when he stuck out his tongue it became clear that its colour had nothing to do with *creme de menthe*.

'Ha-ha-ha', roared the challenger. 'I found half a bottle of green ink and in it went, ha-ha-ha.'

I should mention here that a few weeks later we heard that one of the trainee pilots based at Claresolm had died after a bout of excessive drinking — we were shocked to hear it but certainly not surprised.

We had breakfast (a rather bleary-eyed breakfast) and headed west and south through Glacier National Park, Montana, USA, which was absolutely amazing — great canyons and narrow roads cut into the cliff face. The place was commercialised to a certain extent but in a sensible way — for instance — at every good viewing point there was a big framed sheet of information on all the various landmarks that could be seen. Being servicemen we did not have to pay the toll to get in. Along the road a series of wooden boards warned us not to make friends with the bears that roam this part of the country. The next night we rented a cabin (bungalow) in a place called Coeur D'alene. The next day we went through the most desert-like of barren wildernesses that you could imagine until we got to the Grand Coulee Dam, which was quite amazing. We drove across the top of the dam and the roar of falling water was deafening. A little later we drove on to discover the Dry Falls of the Columbia River, the giant remains of a great prehistoric waterfall. After gaping for some time at this rather wonderful sight we decided we'd better get a move on if we wanted to make Vancouver by nightfall. Speeding west we unfortunately overtook a *police car in a 25mph speed limit area. We didn't notice we were being followed out of town by the cops until they screamed at us with their siren! These Yankee cops took a dim view of our speeding and we didn't feel like arguing as they were both armed with revolvers. They had the last word. 'Guess you'd best foller us into town 'n'see what the judge has to say.' An hour later after our Canadian friend — the guilty driver — had been fined 30 dollars, we carried on with no further hitch.*

Reading this letter, sent to my parents sixty years ago, brings back the action in sharp detail. 'Get out of the car and keep your hands where we can see them.' One of these pale-blue uniformed crooks had his eye on us while the other walked slowly round the car. 'Engine smells mighty hot.' Al explained that we'd come a long way but . . . 'You were doin' pretty near forty comin' through our town, 'n' cutting corners on mountain bends.'

We followed their cruiser back into the so-called town and stopped outside a single storey shack. Al was escorted into what turned out to be a carefully laid trap while the rest of us were told to wait in the car. When Al eventually re-appeared he got back behind the wheel and drove on. 'The judge wanted me to pay three hundred dollars bail. When I told him I didn't have that kind of money he said that you guys should chip in. I said we were trainee pilots based in Canada and you two had come all the way from England on a once-in-a-lifetime visit to the wonderful US-of-A. The judge puffed cigar smoke at me, fixed a date for my trial and finally settled for 30 bucks, a tenth of the asking price, knowing full well that I would never appear before him in his God-forsaken courtroom.'

Twenty years later I watched an American TV comedy series called *Dukes of Hazzard* featuring an evil sheriff called Boss Hogg who used his ill-gotten authority to become fat and rich. I sometimes wonder who that character was based on.

Johnny and I drove from then on. My turn gave little opportunity for speeding as we were caught in a tremendous string of traffic. At about 9pm we reached Vancouver where John and I stayed two nights at the family home of Al Nichol and were shown all the sights of Vancouver. After that we took the steamer to Victoria, the capital of Vancouver Island. Victoria is a very English city. On the steamer we saw some very high-brow English types, easily distinguished by their clothes which were either dark-grey suits or tweed jackets. Another thing that showed them up was that they ate with both knife and fork, not like our Canadian and American friends who cut everything up with knife and fork — switch the fork to the right hand leaving the knife (quite forgotten) with the blade resting on the edge of the plate with the handle on the table. One female, also English, greeted us with the words 'Are you RAF?' pronounced 'rarf'. She told us a bit about Victoria (our immediate destination) and said that she found it very much like England, in fact she might almost be in her home town in Kent! We spent two nights in Victoria in a hotel and went on a tour of the Butchart Gardens, an amazing fifty-acre national park in what was once a limestone quarry that provided raw material for the Butchart cement business.

The woman on the ferry who asked if we were 'rarf' was certainly right when she said that Victoria would remind us of England with its old-fashioned lampposts and hanging flower baskets.

After Victoria we got onto the steamer again and arrived in Seattle USA where we *stayed the night. By 2am the following night we had hitched 400 miles, which seems amazing. We travelled about half that journey with a farmer in a pick-up truck, which is American for an open-backed van. We had two punctures that presented problems seeing that there was only one spare wheel. The following day we left Grants Pass in a lorry on its way to collect some sawn up logs (planks) or as they say here 'lumber'. This guy was very amusing and evidently found Englishmen quite a novelty. He showed us all round the sawmill which was completely constructed of wood and looked as though it had been standing there since the days of the Red Indians, although the machinery seemed very up to date.*

Reading this letter reminds me of gigantic hydraulic jaws lifting tree trunks and dropping them onto a massive saw bench. The din from a mighty circular saw was horrendous. Nobody wore ear protectors and sawdust flew in all directions. One of the workers explained that he had to pay different annual insurance premiums for each of his ten fingers ranging from right-hand thumb in top slot to left-hand little finger at the bottom.

From the mill we were picked up by a typical American man, wife and daughter who took us to Eureka on the coast where they put us up for the night in their house. This chap was a logger or in other words somebody who hauls logs from forest to sawmill. He was his own boss and owned his own truck (lorry) which was an enormous machine complete with water-cooled brakes for going down hills (we were riding in his car by the way). He had been a US Navy pilot during the war and was fascinated when we told him what had brought us to his country. The next day he was going to 'Frisco' (San Francisco) and gave us a lift all the way there (300 miles). This journey was very interesting as it took us to the Redwoods of California where we saw the most enormous trees that you could ever imagine.

Here again my letter omits another overwhelming impression. Until then I always thought that a tree house was something built amongst the branches, but being able to enter a house built inside the hollowed out trunk of a living tree was something else. The forest was dark. We followed signs to the Founder's Tree, the tallest in the world at 364 feet, but the top was out of sight above a dense canopy. Some of these trees were reputed to be 4000 years old. We followed signs to the gigantic stump of a felled redwood and could clearly see more than two thousand annual rings. These rings were marked with dates and labels: Crusades 1095; Magna Carta 1215; Columbus 1492; Pilgrim Fathers 1620; American Independence 1776 — and so on.

At Frisco we said goodbye to our benefactors and spent the night at the YMCA hotel. Two nights were all we could spare during which we went across the Golden Gate Bridge and the Oakland Bay Bridge which is, believe it or not, 8 miles long (everything in the States seems to be the longest widest or highest in the world).

Johnny and I went on a walk downtown and bought cinema tickets. The programme consisted of a series of sleazy black and white movies showing ladies of varying ages removing their clothes. During the interval a man walked up and down the aisle selling pornographic novelties one of which was a pair of dice. 'Number one — meet the lady. Number two — meet the guy. Number three — boy meets girl . . . and if you don't get a thrill by the time you get to number six, then

161

there must be something wrong with your thrill apparatus.'

From Frisco we went to Los Angeles by bus (400 miles) and stayed once again at the YMCA. Hollywood is a suburb of L.A. and is full of beauty parlours, MG and Jaguar cars and film studios. We didn't have much use for the first, second or fourth of these items but did manage to go round the Universal International Studios and saw the street scene used in the film 'High Noon' which, if you remember, was the Western film we saw in Oxford together. We also saw the Lunatic Asylum used in the film 'Harvey' (featuring an invisible rabbit). All these buildings were just fronts, if you went round the back all you could see were props holding the thing up.

We made this tour of the open-air studios in a bus while the driver gave a running commentary. 'Hey folks, look over there.' He leaned out and shouted from his open window. 'Hiya Chill!' An elderly man in cowboy clothes waved back at the bus driver who turned to us and said, 'Folks, that was Chill Wills!' The gasp of surprise made me realise that we were in the presence of a great film star, one that I had never heard of. Now, sixty years after that memorable bus ride, I never miss a movie on TV that has that old-timer with his battered hat and words of home-spun philosophy. The bus drove past a corral of horses and the driver pointed. 'Take a good look folks, that's Francis, he's the 1951 Picture Animal of the Year award winner.' This time I knew what he was talking about as Johnny and I had seen this witty, deep-voiced animal in a film called *Francis Goes to the Races* in a Red Deer cinema. At the time we didn't know that Francis the Talking Mule had already made three films for International and would go on to delight audiences for a further five years.

Before leaving Los Angeles we visited the pagoda-like Grauman's Chinese Theatre on Hollywood Boulevard and walked over the handprints, signature and footprints of Shirley Temple and many other film stars imprinted in concrete on the pavement outside. Johnny and I had seen Chill and Francis, we had trodden on Shirley's footprints but little did we know that very soon we would be kissing the fragrant cheek of another rising star.

By this time most of our two weeks were up so we went by bus to Reno (our first step home). At Reno we rang John's uncle. An hour later a shooting brake arrived piloted by the uncle's black stooge who drove us to *Lake Tahoe where the uncle managed a posh hotel. The road took us up to 9,000 feet and we were amused to think that, had we gone just 1000 feet higher, we would (by Air Force regulations) have had to turn on the oxygen! The name of this hotel was Cal-Neva Lodge situated on the border of California and Nevada (the state boundary was a line marked on the bottom of the swimming pool). The uncle, complete with white scarf, white shoes and blazer, offered us rooms (normally 20 dollars a night) but we were too pressed for time to accept.*

Johnny's uncle, who had changed his surname from Rose to Ross, welcomed his long-lost nephew with open arms but was disappointed that we couldn't spare the time to take advantage of his generous offer. He stood between us and said, 'You guys ready for this? Care to meet the Marilyn Munro of the future?' He led us to the swimming pool and there she was. Abbe Lane didn't disclose her age but I later discovered she was two years older than me — and married less than twelve months before to an aging bandleader called Xavier Cugat. When she got up from her poolside towel I found myself looking at the top half of her navel just visible above the waistline of her two-piece swimming costume. An obliging waiter fetched a canvas chair and Ross told us to stand either side of her while he took a photograph. 'One to show your grandchildren in years to come.'

After the photo Abbe stood up and gave both Johnny and me a peck on the cheek. 'You boys coming to my show tonight?'

At the cabaret that evening Xavier Cugat exuded vitality with his pencil moustache, red jacket, bow tie, oily black hair, permanent smile and was surrounded by trombonists and clarinet players. Abbe emerged from behind a pillar, finger on chin, shimmering and sexy in a close-fitting green dress and, looking for all the world like that no-good serpent that beguiled Adam and Eve in the Garden of Eden. She sang *Eso es el Amor* and I didn't need to understand Spanish to know what she meant.

After seeing the floor show we were driven back to Reno to catch a northbound Greyhound bus. From Reno we travelled night and day, north and east through mountains deserts forests etc until we finally arrived at Penhold, two weeks older and, I think, very much wiser and certainly very exhausted.

11

Safely back at Penhold, night flying was next on the agenda. Sandwiches and coffee in the crew room brought a strange sense of adventure and camaraderie: orange flames from exhaust pipes, rows of lights marking the edge of invisible tarmac and sometimes a moon to show the hangars in silhouette. Flying away from base we used our maps. Roads and railways could be identified by the moving headlights of cars and trains. Lakes glinted in the moonlight. Towns like Red Deer and Calgary were carpets studded with points of light where cars moved like fireflies between double lines of street lights. Not getting lost was uppermost but if all else failed there was always the radio compass — tune it to home base and a dial on the dashboard swung to show the way.

Dear Mother and Father
We are nearing the end of our night flying, it really has been quite an experience, particularly on one occasion two nights ago when I lost control after landing and ended up about 25 yards off in the grass to the left

of the runway. *Believe me, being towed back to the hangars behind a tractor is highly demoralising. I must have started something as last night while, I was away on a solo nav trip the APO, with whom I went on leave, had similar trouble — he managed to stay on the runway but bent an undercarriage leg and a wingtip. A little later one of the Canadians ran off the end of the runway! This morning I had the first of my instrument flying tests, which I managed to pass. Instrument flying is done with the cockpit windows covered with a big canvas hood so that you can't see out — this is to simulate cloud flying. The test consists of take-off (using the gyro compass to keep straight) climbing, turning and spinning. Landing is done by the examiner who sits in the front cockpit and has been quietly writing comments about my flying. Early next week comes the biggest test so far, known as Harvard Handling. After that it will be nothing but instrument flying and formation.*

While learning how to fly on instruments I began to understand the meaning of G — the initial letter of Gravity. If you swing a bucket of water fast enough over your head the water stays in the bucket even when it's upside down in the same way that G force keeps a pilot's bottom firmly pressed into the seat when looping the loop or pulling a tight turn. Under the hood my bottom felt as if it was pressing down, then lifting, slewing sideways and none of these sensations bore any resemblance to what was really happening to the aeroplane. By the time I had finished the instrument course I knew how to fly straight and level, loop the loop, recover from unusual attitudes and after a total of twenty hours and fifteen minutes of weird sensations under that hood I was able to ignore the seat of my pants.

I now have 140 hours and should have about 200 by the end of the course (Dec 18th if I pass all the flying and ground school tests). Today I watched one of the junior course APOs doing his first solo, his instructor was standing next to me looking rather nervous; soon the instructor heaved a sigh of relief, the APO had his tie docked and everything worked out happily. Last weekend we went to Calgary to the YWCA dance, which was very good. They put on a floor show for our entertainment, which was cut short by one of the girls fainting in the middle of it, she was all right later though. Unfortunately I left the address of

Mrs C.S. Lee back at camp so my visit to her will have to be postponed (we are 90 miles from Calgary). There are rumours that we will be getting our wings at the end of this course before we go on to AFS (advanced). We finish AFS in April after which time I hope for 2 weeks leave (they don't know what a fortnight is in Canada) in and around Darlington. The weather is just starting to turn cold — apparently the Red Indians are saying that it is going to be a very cold winter although the afternoons at the moment are still quite sunny. Last weekend we went to Calgary (another invasion of the YWCA by Penhold) for the usual reason, the Y dance. I met a Chinese girl who knew Hankow and Shanghai, Ewo Brewery etc. This was highly interesting even though China (as yet) is not included in the radius of my globetrotting. On Saturday afternoon I rang up Mrs Lee without success as they were out. When I tried again on Sunday afternoon Mrs Lee said they were just on their way to a christening but told me to come round at 4pm and make myself at home in the house, which I did. They arrived back at about 4.45, Ma, Pa and 3 little girls between the ages of about 7 and 12. They hadn't been home 15 minutes when they *had me involved in one of those tantalising games when you have to roll coloured balls into holes on a sloping board. The first round I scored 550 which had them all swooning — the second round was a really prize one as I scored the amazing total of 10 and consequently lost the game. Mr Lee is an oil prospector working in and around Calgary; from all accounts they find Canada a highly delightful place to live in but I still think there is nothing to beat 'Old England'. Their house is very close to Currie Field it is a pity I didn't know of their existence before I moved to Penhold. One of our main recreations in Red Deer is Billiards — it seems that Englishmen are the only ones who play the game as Canadians always play snooker. Billiards therefore is a novelty and we usually have a large audience who find it entertaining to watch this alien game!*

We all make mistakes. One day I drove our Ford into Red Deer, a rapidly-expanding town in the grip of an oil boom. Our Harvards burned gasoline at a mere forty gallons an hour but in Red Deer the earth was positively bubbling with the stuff from which petrol is made. Off-duty drillers and riggers arrived in battered trucks in search of amusement and I quickly learned Rule Number One when parking. As a child my mother constantly reminded me to think of others, and I thought of her every time I parked in Red Deer. Never apply the handbrake because others might also need space to park. Going bumper to bumper and gently shoving a whole line of cars to make your own space was standard practice. I managed to park (as described) and walked off to buy whatever it was I had come for, got back to the car, successfully restarted the car but managed to stall the engine at the first set of traffic lights. I then proceeded to run down the battery trying to restart. I was expecting the driver behind to honk and shout but instead he got out of his battered vehicle and came over. 'Need a shove?' When I said yes he walked back to his truck, closed the gap with a shattering jolt, waited for the lights to turn green and pushed me down the street bumper-to-bumper. What a helpful man! I engaged second gear and let out the clutch — not even a splutter. He pushed me at increasing speed through the streets of Red Deer, and continued to shove while I selected different gears to no avail. After ten minutes of this I suddenly realised what was wrong. I switched on the ignition and roared happily away with a cheery wave of thanks. Back at

Penhold I noticed another dent on our rear fender.

Looking back on my fourteen months spent in Canada there was seldom a day when I didn't have something to either laugh at or else frighten me half to death. I remember Johnny Rose coming into the crew room after a solo flight looking like a burnt chicken with hair singed and eyebrows gone. We crowded round to hear what had happened. He'd had trouble starting. The normal starting procedure for a Harvard before switching on the ignition was to pump up petrol with the hand-operated wobble pump, inject primer fuel into the top cylinders by pushing a knob in and out marked Kigas (never more than four times), engage the starter and switch on the ignition. Johnny had done all these things several times and in the right order but still no joy. He tried again and again until finally: wobble-wobble-wobble-wobble-wobble-wobble. Kigas plunger: one-two-three-four-five-six-seven-eight-nine — and he went on pumping Kigas until the sheer pressure of the stuff in the top cylinders stopped him pushing any more. That should do it, he thought. Engage the starter motor, turn the engine, switches on — BANG. The engine ejaculated a gigantic tongue of flame that shot back from the exhaust pipe, spiralled into the open cockpit and took poor Johnny totally by surprise. His eyebrows took a long time to grow back much to the delight of the Red Deer girls.

We had another Johnny on the course, Johnny Cramb, who made an even more dramatic entrance into the crew room after a training flight. When World War Three didn't happen Johnny Cramb went on to enjoy a long career as an airline pilot, but it makes me smile whenever I try to imagine how his passengers might have reacted if they had been able to see their captain, white as a sheet and waddling through the door of our crew room with his parachute over his shoulder. You didn't need to be a doctor to see that the man wasn't feeling good. As he tried to make a bee-line for the lavatory somebody shouted after him, 'What's up Johnny?'

He turned and spoke through ashen lips. 'It's true.'

'What's true?'

'It's true, that's all. What they say is true.'

'For Christ's sake Johnny, what's true?' We gathered round to find out.

'I never believed it until now, but when you're about to die you shit yourself.'

After he'd cleaned himself up, Johnny was kind enough to tell us what had happened to him. At the end of an aerobatic session with his instructor he was told to climb to the regulation height and put the aircraft into a spin. At 8,000 feet he closed the throttle, eased back the stick, gave it full right rudder and went whirling down towards the ground in a text-book spin. After half a dozen turns his instructor told him to recover so he applied full left rudder and eased the stick progressively forward. I knew exactly what he was talking about when he told us that the spin whirled faster and faster. When his instructor yelled 'JUMP' Johnny undid his harness, disconnected his radio lead, slid back the canopy and had one leg over the side when the Harvard suddenly jerked out of the spin. Johnny fell back into the cockpit and sat uncomfortably for the rest of the flight.

My tooth was hurting like hell, one of the big ones at the back. Sixty years later, whenever I push my tongue into the gap I picture a middle-aged Army dentist in brown uniform. He'd been brought in to do the job with the help of a rather dishy French Canadian nurse. My rotting tooth had little to show for itself above the gum but the roots proved long, strong, twisted and well embedded. It was a struggle, not for me but for the dentist who probed, swore, levered and pulled. The tooth came out in bits after heavy blows with a hammer and chisel but the discomfort that followed was made tolerable by the dentist's Brigitte Bardot look-alike who invited me to drop my trousers: 'For ze Pennicilin injection in ze 'ip.'

Before leaving England all RAF trainee pilots had been promoted from Aircraftsman Second Class (AC2) to Acting Pilot Officer on Probation (APO). We were officers and would remain so as long as we stayed on the course and qualified for our Pilot's Badge or Wings. Now, however, we were attached to the Canadian Air Force where things were different. All Canadian, Dutch and Danish students had the rank of Cadet while the Italians and French were either Corporals or Sergeants. This didn't cause any problem as we all shared the same billets and relaxed together in the students' mess. To all intents and purposes we were all cadets — no problem until one day a junior female RCAF officer ticked off one of the RAF students for not saluting her. The RAF man politely pointed out that as an acting Pilot Officer he only saluted ranks senior to himself.

Several different nationalities all trying to sing from the same hymn sheet sometimes presented problems. One of our first tasks in Ground School was to learn the Phonetic Alphabet, a string of badly chosen words that are now totally obsolete: Able, Baker, Charlie, Dog, Easy, Fox, George, How, Item, Jig,

King, Love, Mike, Nan, Oboe, Peter, Queenie, Roger, Sugar, Tare, Uncle, Victor, William, X-Ray, Yoke, Zebra. When our instructor reckoned we had memorised this infamous collection he went through the alphabet, testing us in turn by pointing to each of us in no particular order. Able, Baker, Charlie, Dog, Easy . . . by now his finger was pointing at a Frenchman who hesitated. I could read his mind, I knew what was coming and I could see the agony on the poor chap's face. He knew what the correct word sounded like but . . . when he blurted out a four letter word (instead of FOX) he received a prolonged round of applause.

We all loved the French but how I regret not having shared some childhood memories of WW2 with them. Their country had been liberated from Nazi occupation a mere seven years before and I would have dearly liked to know more about what that was like, although it might not have been a popular subject with them. One of my French friends, let's call him Anton, was completely crazy about anything to do with aviation, he showed us photographs of an aircraft he had built and flown himself, with an undercarriage built from crashed Spitfires' tail wheels and an air-cooled engine salvaged from a wrecked car. For reasons I never discovered our superiors wanted to see the back of him and soon found an excuse. While preparing for a solo flight Anton went through the normal routine — he started the engine, ran it to full power with wheel chocks in place to test his magnetos and was about to taxi towards the runway when he saw an instructor sitting in the rear seat of the aircraft parked next to him, pointing at his Harvard and gesticulating wildly. The baggage door on the side of Anton's aircraft, obviously not properly latched down, had been lifted by the spiralling prop-wash and was sticking out like a shelf. The Frenchman throttled back to tick-over but the shelf remained sticking out, held in the horizontal position by its click-up hinges. Anton got out, climbed down, banged the door shut and climbed back in again. Was it his lack of English that made him ignorant of the golden rule? Never leave the cockpit of an aircraft with the engine running. Disobeying that rule (or so they said) was the reason why Anton was immediately chopped from the course and sent back to France, which I thought was a bit heavy handed.

On one memorable Saturday morning, Mike Massey woke us up very early to say that last night he had made an important telephone call. All four members of the Ford

V8 Syndicate had been invited to spend the day on a remote farm owned by his uncle and aunt. I was thrilled at the prospect, a chance to witness life on a Canadian farm; perhaps it would be a farm like the one described in A.G. Street's Farmer's Glory.

We skipped breakfast and had to wait for our local gas station to open. After filling up and picking up a map, we zig-zagged for hours along those dusty north-south and east-west tracks bordering one-square-mile 'sections' of prairie that we knew so well from the air. Ninety miles later we found the track leading to the farm and were greeted with open arms by Mike Massey's jovial aunt who hugged us all in turn. 'You boys must be starving. Come in and get washed up.' I took my turn in the bathroom, washing my hands with an unscented hunk of soap. Sitting around a well-scrubbed table, each with a T-bone steak overlapping its wooden platter, I asked about the soap. Massey's aunt had made it from beef tallow. 'Add water, boil it up and then stir in your caustic soda.'

After lunch we piled onto the farmer's truck and drove across sparse pasture to inspect a herd of white-faced beef cattle. For me it was a wonderful moment of peace: no cars, no aeroplanes — just the modest voice of the farmer proudly explaining to us that all these animals were descended from his highly-prized Hereford bull. On the drive back to Penhold I found myself envying the lifestyle I had just witnessed — my ambition from boyhood was to be a farmer. My grandfather came from a long line of farmers so it was in my blood. I had seen Canadian agriculture from the air, tractors ploughing, huge herds of cattle and grain silos by the railroad and now I had seen it from ground level. But I also wanted to fly.

Some of our flights were routine almost to the point of boredom — looking back I'm amazed to think that it could be — boring I mean. We learned how to fly down radio beams that criss-crossed Canada: dit-dah in your earphones to the right, dah-dit to the left of the invisible beam and a steady note when you were on the beam and finally a cone of silence when you passed over the transmitter. Radio Range, as it was called, had been invented by the Luftwaffe to find targets like Coventry and Plymouth seven years before. I spent a total of twenty hours and fifteen minutes learning this skill. I was glad when it was over because next on the agenda was Formation Flying.

For reasons that I've never fully understood, qualified pilots must be able to fly dangerously close to each other. When formation flying started we were encouraged do what I had tried to do over Sylvan Lake. 'Fly close to the guy next to you. If you can't see the hole in his ear you're not close enough.' Was my instructor exaggerating? He must have been because we all wore canvas helmets that covered our ears. Finger-Left or Finger-Right — that describes how four aircraft fly in formation. Extend your left hand, palm down with thumb tucked under; now imagine that your four fingernails are flying in formation. Your longest finger is Number One, he's the leader. On his right (your index finger) is Number Two. On the leader's left is Number Three followed by your little finger Number Four. The runway is wide enough for only two planes to take off together, so Number Three must wait for the runway to clear before he can lead Number Four to catch the others who by now are fast disappearing into the distance. I liked being Number Three best as I enjoyed the chase. These formations always had an instructor on board at least one of the aircraft.

Once correctly formed up in Close Formation, all four planes would be close enough to be able to read hand signals. This may sound dangerous but, although the speeds were relatively high, the Harvard, unlike a car, can't cause a shunt by suddenly jamming on its brakes. Number One was responsible for navigation and keeping a good lookout while everybody else kept his eyes glued to the plane next door, watching for hand signals and practising turns to right and left. Sometimes we would spread out into Battle Formation, which was more complicated especially in a turn because Number Four and Number Three were supposed to slide under the others and take up position on the inside of the turn. After twelve hours of this and a few near misses we became quite good at flying in formation.

We still spent half of every day in Ground School. Lessons included how to survive after parachuting into the Canadian wilderness, the science behind how and why clouds form, improving our speed at sending and receiving Morse Code by buzzer or Aldis lamp.

I have never taken sport very seriously, and I was in good company. The RCAF's principle sport was drinking, maybe because the climate was too hot in summer and too cold in winter for anything more strenuous. We never played football or cricket but we did play snooker, also table tennis every evening in the mess at which fellow APO David Courtier-Dutton had an un-returnable serve due to the incredible amount of spin he managed to put on the ball. Skeet shooting happened every Wednesday afternoon for anyone interested and was something I looked forward to. A Skeet is a small disk shaped like a Frisbee made from fragile material that breaks up in mid-air if winged by a shotgun pellet, or else bursts into a puff of black smoke if the shooter scores a direct hit with all 340 lead pellets from a twelve-bore shotgun. The English call it clay pigeon shooting. Let's pretend it's Wednesday afternoon: first comes a pep talk from our skeet coach: 'Skeet shooting is a recreational activity for civilians, but for you lot it's a skill that could save your life. If you can master the art of breaking clay disks in flight you should be able to do the same to an enemy pilot when World War Three breaks out, and break out it will mark my words. This is why we're here this afternoon. In front of you is the tower. Skeets will be catapulted out of that window near the top of the tower. After each shot you move to the next firing point, this way you will have a go at every angle — right side, straight in front and left side. Keep both eyes open at all times. Never aim directly at a moving target. Shout PULL when you're ready. Any questions?' I can't say I was an expert at skeet shooting but the advice to aim in front of a moving target saved me from disaster about a year later (after I had left the RAF) when I was invited to a shoot in Scotland. Walking with my companions in line abreast across a stubble field, a hare got up and ran in front of us parallel to the line. I was walking next to a highly experienced and trusted gamekeeper who addressed me urgently, 'Your shot sir, your shot.' I raised my twelve-bore but hesitated. Two Labrador dogs were in hot pursuit, inches away from the hare. 'Your shot sir!' Although I already knew the names of the two dogs I was being reminded by aristocratic screams from the far end of the line: 'Come back Archie, come here Stanley!'. Determined not to kill Angela's precious pets I aimed so far in front of the hare that I was certain to miss the lot. I fired. Both dogs lived and, to my great surprise and hankering regret, the hare died instantly.

Friday 24th October 1953

Dear Mother and Father
Thank you very much for the letter, you seem to be leading quite an enjoyable session of holidays. I have taken three final flying tests. Navigation, Instruments and Harvard Handling, and have managed to pass them OK. I still have the Radio Range test, which entails a different method of

getting to the airfield when visibility is too low to do it visually, and my last test will be Formation Flying, about the most hair-raising of the lot. Our final exams in Ground School start on November 3rd so I am swotting up at full throttle for what I think is the highest fence on the course. I must say that I am pining to continue with my farming. I was wondering if you would think it a good idea if, after I have completed my NDA course and had gained further experience after that, if I took a job similar to the enclosed advert taken from the Farmers Weekly — what exactly the work would entail is difficult to say but it would be an excellent reference for when I returned to England after 4 or 5 years. — anyway, it was just an idea (of course it need not be Mau Mau land as there are similar jobs going in other colonies). On Monday week we become the Senior Course and become in charge of what is known as 'The Cadet Organisation'. I have been appointed as a Flight Commander and editor of our magazine, which goes by the name of 'Top Sec.' The weather we are told is typical of the Fall which, being interpreted, means Autumn. We have finished our solo flying now until we start formation flying. There is a school of thought that says we will be inclined to become more dangerous now that we have passed the majority of our flying tests. In my next letter you will hear the verdict of my final ground school exams and after that, if by any chance I pass them, it will be plain sailing until we get onto our little 600 knot jobs. From all accounts a jet is very simple to fly except for landing — the landing speed is 120 knots as opposed to 80 in the Harvard. Our car still runs as reliably as ever (touch wood) and is our sole means of transport into Red Deer. Complete brake failure managed to put it nose-down in rather a deep ditch and a week passed before we could extract it.

For some reason I failed to tell the truth, the whole truth and nothing but ... Maybe I should have written: Dear Mother and Father. I was driving our precious Ford with my three co-owners on board, careered into a gigantic roadside ditch on a Sunday afternoon and when I tried to drive out of it the back wheels dug in axle-deep and we had to abandon the car. In the days that followed the four anxious owners persuaded their instructors to let them fly over the offending ditch to make sure the car was still there. On Friday afternoon I sighed with relief, below my wing there it was — our precious Ford V8 just as we had left it. On Saturday morning the four of us, complete with tow-rope, drove to the spot in a borrowed car and looked down into the ditch. Believe me, there is no sight so depressing in this world as the empty space left by a stolen car. The ditch was empty. The Mounties always get their man, this time they got our car. In the RCMP office we paid a painful sum to retrieve one shabby, brakeless Ford V8 from amongst an interesting array of captured vehicles.

I can't imagine driving a car with the controls on the right-hand side and, as for driving on the left-hand side of the road, only a lunatic would do it — and that's for sure. Well, it is studying time now, so you'll have to wait for the next thrilling instalment featuring my exam results.
With love from James

December 1953

Dear Mother and Father
It seems that I haven't written for quite a time — time enough for quite a bit of news. First of all, thank you very much for the socks. I wore them the evening they arrived at a big formal dance to celebrate the opening of our new mess at Penhold. I asked a

girl who is at a nurses' training school in Red Deer who I have known for a few weeks — a good time was had by all. I went down to see the Lee's not so long ago in Calgary and was with them for a day. We went for a drive to Bearspaw Dam, which is one of the sights of Calgary, and then back home to do some carpentry on the basement that Pa Lee is making into a playroom for his 3 girls. That night Mrs Lee and myself went to a hockey game (hockey means ice-hockey when in Canada). We saw the Edmonton Eskimos beat the Calgary Stampeders 7–3, which rather disgusted all the Calgary spectators. We were taken to the game by an ex-British army colonel and during the three intervals in the game we met all manner of county types from England. Canadian ice hockey is quite a rough game and frequently you notice players tripping up their opponents behind the backs of the two referees. One player somehow got an opponent's stick tucked under his arm and refused to let go in spite of much tugging from the other party and some fierce umbrella swats from an old lady sitting close to the barrier.

At 10am last Tuesday I was seen 'fighting me case' in the Red Deer court room. Here is the story: on the night of

December the 5th at approximately 8.15pm in the city of Red Deer a collision occurred between a taxi and a private car at the intersection of Rose street and 47th Avenue (I expect by now you are wondering how this involved me — that's simple — I was riding in the taxi with my nurse friend Jean, see above) We were going east and the other car was going south and each reckoned that the other should have stopped. Anyway, this was all some time ago and I had almost forgotten about it until I received a phone call from the taxi driver to meet him, with Jean, before the session in court was due to start — 10am. We met down in Red Deer and went to see the taxi driver's lawyer, in his office, who tried to jog our memories. Well we went to court and had to wait for three other cases to be completed, these were: speeding, drunk in charge and carrying opened bottles of booze in a car.

The court case before ours remains clear in my memory. The wisecracking judge sat behind his raised desk. A dishevelled man faced him. The judge put his hands together and asked the man to state his name and occupation. 'Okay so you're a fisherman. What's your address?'

'My car.'

'Come on man, where do you live'

'In my car.'

'Do you admit that when you were stopped by the Mounties they found an open bottle of rye whisky in your car?'

'Yes sir.'

'Then no doubt you will also admit you are guilty as charged.'

'No sir.'

'How come? Explain yourself man.'

'I was at home.'

'Don't play with me clever guy. You were in your car, right?'

'But my car is also my home and thanks to God nobody's yet made a law against a hard working fisherman having a swig of rye in his own home.'

The judge smiled. 'I guess the Mounties did a better fishing job than you ever did. Fined ten dollars. Next case.'

Our case came next. I was called to give evidence and Jean gave me a reassuring wave. I told the court that the taxi crashed into another vehicle but I hadn't the faintest idea whose fault it was because I wasn't looking out of the window. The judge glared at me over his half-moon specs. 'Young man, if you hadn't been canoodlin' with that young lady on the back seat of that taxi you might be helpin' this court with some evidence instead of wasting our valuable time.'

Unfortunately we lost our case. After a lot of wrangling the taxi driver was found guilty of not observing the right of way and was fined $10, he also had to pay $166 for a new door for the other car. Our car flaked out the other day and we have since sold it for $40, which wasn't too bad considering we had to be towed into town. The trouble was that one of the owners forgot to let the water out of the radiator one night and it froze solid — this caused water to leak all over the place after it thawed out, including the inside of the engine. The engine was going OK the day before we sold it, but with rather high water consumption.

Well here's wishing you the best for Xmas, in case I don't write again. It's a pity there were just 4 little mice to devour the Xmas goodies instead of 6. I was thinking of you on the day. Doubtless an RCAF Xmas has its unusual points so. I'll tell you all about it. Can't think of anything more to say except MERRY CHRISTMAS!!! about a hundred times. Thank you again for all the presents. Much love from James.

Flying Officer Robertson's favourite hobby was flying upside down. This was an attitude frequently adopted for a few seconds while looping the loop, but Robertson liked to prolong the agony. Knowing this I was glad I wasn't on his list, but when my regular instructor went on leave I got Robertson for aerobatic practice. Sure enough, as soon as we had cleared the circuit and climbed away from the airfield, Robertson flipped the Harvard onto its back. Fortunately I had already made sure my harness was tight, just as well because I found myself hanging upside down with all my weight supported by webbing straps over — no, under — my shoulders. 'Gravity, that's what we're up against Stevenson. It's gravity that feeds our engine so keep wobbling the wobble-pump otherwise our engine will wonder why it has nothing to drink.' I wobbled frantically while a cloud of gravity-free dust rose in front of my eyes. A forgotten screwdriver moved slowly in front of my face before clattering into the Perspex dome above — or below — the top of my head. No, I have to say that I never shared Robertson's enthusiasm for inverted flight.

Flying Officer Spencer ended my course on Harvards with a lesson on the art of landing without flaps. I managed to survive and did it solo on 10 December 1953.

So that was it. After flying for 194 hours and 45 minutes on the Yellow Peril I was still alive, looking forward to a short Christmas leave and about to be posted to the Jet School at Portage la Prairie near Winnipeg in the province of Manitoba.

Dear Mother and Father, Hew and John.
Thank you all very much for the Christmas presents. The hankies are almost too good to blow my nose on and the address book is most useful to record the multi-addresses I've collected since I have been here in Canada. I'm afraid my Xmas card is rather dull compared to the one you sent me. My Xmas presents will be rather small this year, and probably won't have arrived on time. I hope you can wait till Easter for something a little better. I have been quite busy lately with our magazine 'Top Sec', which I hope will appear next week. It really is quite a job but it will be most satisfying to see it completed. I think in my last letter I told you that our next station would be Gimli — we have since found out that it will be Portage la Prairie (a typical Canadian name) also in Manitoba (like Gimli). It is situated about 60 miles west of Winnipeg and about 100 miles from the

US border. I had a letter from Ronald the other day (with birthday greetings) in which he described the unbearable heat of such places as Bombay. I think it would be highly satisfactory if we could arrange to exchange temperatures for a few days, because here at the moment the temp. seldom rises above freezing, which is nothing compared to what the winter has in store for us — it has to be at least 50F below freezing before you can get a Canadian to remark on the coolness of the atmosphere! 90 below is by no means unheard of in Manitoba. I am so glad the photos arrived safely. I was given some bad advice regarding postage rates and realised it would be going by sea the day after I posted them. We will get our wings either during or after the Advanced course at Portage. We can hardly wait to tackle jets. If we are an average course we will all have flown solo by the time we have 9 hours dual — quite a difference when compared to my 25 before going solo on the Harvard. The last flying test I took was formation flying. I was lucky on this test as I was flying solo and being marked by an instructor sitting in the back seat of the aircraft flying next to me, so close that I could almost tell how my marks were going by the expression on his face — he must have had a stomach ache at the time because I passed! When flying in close formation you have to keep your eyes glued on the plane on which you are formating — edging up as close as you consider safe. Battle formation is more spread out and is therefore easier, but turning is like a complicated square dance movement, with everyone sliding under each other to regain their allotted places in a rather unnerving manner. On Wednesday we have a graduation mess dinner (bow-ties and white shirts with best blue).

On Christmas Eve we went to a carol service in the station chapel and sang all the old favourites and a lot more besides. After the service we were given a lift down town by the Padre for Midnight Communion. During the service a terrific wind got up and by the end of the service we were having a regular blizzard with Christmas day just 90 minutes old. We all piled into the Padre's car (all eight of us) and drove back to Penhold — not on the road, but on a sheet of ice covering it — a most unusual Christmas we were in for at this rate. I may as well explain what our plans were for 'Yule'. Several families in Red Deer had been asked to be put in touch with NATO students at Penhold so that Christmas dinners could be had with Canadian families. This was an excellent idea and John Rose and myself were duly fixed up. At one o'clock we were met at the main gate and taken to their house. Mrs was from Sunderland and was pure Geordie and very amusing indeed to talk to. There were two children, Judy aged 9 and Bill aged 5. Well, we talked non-stop till about 5 o'clock when we had a complete Xmas dinner with everything double size. Later that evening we went round to see Ken Korven and his wife. K.K is the senior weather forecaster at Penhold (civilian) and we had booze and turkey sandwiches with them. At about 2am the party broke up and we were driven back to Penhold having had a most enjoyable Xmas — we talked about everything from the Northern Echo to Durham Cathedral. On Boxing Day evening we travelled down to Calgary and boarded the train to take us to Portage la Prairie — and here is the answer to the mystery question. The irregularity in the writing is caused by the swaying, yawing, pitching and rolling of the train. We are due in Portage at 4.40pm. It is now (after putting my watch on one hour) 12 midday. We are all very impatient to get to AFS

— doing slow rolls at a height of 6 miles above the earth will be quite a novel experience. We had our final Mess Dinner some time ago — the 20 survivors of our course and all our instructors — both flying and ground. It was a formal do with bow ties etc. After dinner the Groupy made a speech and gave away the graduation certificates. We each had our photos taken in the act. The RCAF send a copy of the photo to the local paper of each student's home town, so be prepared for a sudden drop in circulation.

I hope you had a very happy Christmas and that basting the turkey did not present too much trouble. Do write and tell me all about it. I sent you a rather dull present by sea and I'm afraid it will arrive after the term has started but you will be able to send some of it off to H & J — now you are wondering what it is but you will just have to wait and see — though it isn't very exciting. My new address will be Officers' Mess, RCAF Portage la Prairie, Manitoba. At the moment we are travelling east across the prairies — everywhere I look there is nothing but snow and sunshine. The few trees to be seen along the railroad are covered in thick hoar frost, and I notice that the telephone wires look like thick white ropes — thick with frozen snow. Well I have run out of news so a happy New Year to all. Love from James. (posted Winnipeg 29 Dec 1953)

12

We were warned about the cold and for good reason. Indoors everything was centrally heated and very hot but, when out of doors, Manitoba in January 1954 seemed like the coldest place on earth. Never touch anything made of metal unless you're wearing gloves or you'll stick. Keep your ears covered because frostbite is considered a self-inflicted wound. Tiny icicles form inside your nose with every intake of breath and your hair freezes if you don't wear a cap. Snow covers the ground in all directions but at least the frozen crust on top stops you sinking in. The runways are cleared by self-propelled ploughs that throw snow sideways in small avalanches. There was, however, a limit below which even Canadians were forced to respect: when the mercury dropped to 30 below zero Fahrenheit flying was cancelled because ground crew were unable to work outside.

In 1954, Portage la Prairie seemed to me like a two-horse town in the middle of nowhere, but thankfully only sixty miles from Winnipeg, the capital city of Manitoba. No.2 Advanced Flying Training had quite recently reopened but long before it had been home to No.14 Elementary Flying School, part of the British Commonwealth Air Training Plan using Harvards to train pilots during WW2.

Never mind the history. I'm proud to say that now I was a wide-eyed pupil at the recently-opened JET SCHOOL. An Air Force bus took us to the airfield. Apart from the cold, the first thing I noticed on alighting was the smell of burning paraffin from Rolls Royce Nene jet engines, not to mention a thrilling sound — a strange whining from not very far away. Whenever I find myself in a modern airport I breathe in and imagine myself back in what for me was the most exciting school in the world. Snow was everywhere. Heavy falls kept the snowploughs busy, flinging white avalanches sideways to keep the runways clear.

Squadron Leader Mullen gave us an introductory pep talk: 'Gentlemen, I hope you've all settled in to your new quarters. Welcome to the jet age and the T33 Canadair Silver Star. You're going to be fighter pilots — every man a tiger.' I christened him 'Tiger' Mullen, and the nickname stuck.

Before we were allowed to go anywhere near the cockpit we were fitted with back-type parachutes (worn like a haversack). A lengthy lecture on survival followed: 'I expect you've all noticed the emergency oxygen bottle attached to your parachute harness — it's there to keep you alive should you eject at high altitude. Yes, I said eject — no more climbing onto the wing and throwing yourself off. To escape from a burning Silver Star you have to first blast off the canopy — your instructor will show how. Abandon ship. Okay, you've unplugged your radio lead, plugged your oxygen tube into the bottle, the canopy has gone and now it's your turn to go. You and your seat blast off into the atmosphere. You are strapped into that seat and falling. You must undo your straps, kick yourself clear and keep calm. You're at forty thousand feet. The temperature is one hundred degrees below freezing. Pull the ripcord now and you'll be solid ice before you hit the ground. From forty thousand you have to free fall for three minutes. Time it on your watch. Pull the ripcord after three minutes and hope you don't land in some remote wilderness where nobody can find you. Canada is a big country, that's why we've developed the seat cushion — and for God's sake don't forget to dog-clip it onto your parachute harness first-thing when you enter the cockpit. That cushion attached to your butt can save your goddam life. It's all perfectly simple.' It didn't sound perfectly simple to me but who was I to argue? However, I did know something about a completely different type of ejector seat, the Martin Baker, a design that had been saving British lives since 1949. The British way of abandoning a jet in flight was to reach over your shoulder, pull some kind of blind over your face and hey presto you landed safely — no unstrapping yourself from the seat in mid-air, no timed free-falling, and no ripcord to pull.

The American-inspired seat cushion was something else. Before every flight I made sure that it was securely dog-clipped to my parachute harness — just in case. It was indeed a cushion, without it my head wouldn't have shown above the parapet. Why did it have a zip running round the top? Open it and let me show you what's inside: an all-metal Hornet .22 rifle for killing edible animals, all in bits so it fits inside the cushion; a small mirror with a hole in the middle and a sighting loop attached — for flashing reflected sunlight at high-flying aircraft; fishing gear, matches, survival rations, spare socks, compass, first aid, food tins, survival booklet, knife, water-bladder, gloves, blanket — they were all there, crammed into that very comforting cushion.

My eyelids would begin to droop during long-winded lectures on how to survive in the northern wastes of Canada, but I was always wide-awake for training films showing what happens to the chap who wanders away from his crashed aircraft, does everything wrong and is never found because he forgets to mark out a sign for searching aircraft. The splendid survivor, on the other hand, shows us how it should be done. In spite of a sprained ankle he opens his seat cushion, assembles his Hornet rifle, shoots a co-operative rabbit, lights a fire, eats a hearty meal, keeps warm, catches a rainbow trout for breakfast, uses his heliograph mirror and is rescued after three days by a sledge, a team of huskies, a dishy nurse and a doctor — all dropped from the sky by parachute.

I was itching to get my hands on a jet and, on 12 January 1954, my wish was granted. Before taking me up for my first flight, Flying Officer Brown explained what was going to happen: 'This is a different kind of aeroplane, Stevenson — no propeller, no vibration, two and a half tons of thrust up your backside and more than 600 gallons of juice to keep you airborne for three hours, that's if you're careful. Shall we give it a go?'

I picked up my parachute, walked out across the snow and looked round the aircraft with Brown talking me through the external pre-take-off checks. I put on both my helmets, my back-type parachute and climbed aboard using a special hook-on ladder. Brown climbed up behind me and pointed to the canopy ejection lever. He ran through the abandon-aircraft procedure and made sure I plugged my oxygen pipe into its corresponding socket. First impressions: tiny cockpit and, wonder of wonders, the aircraft was horizontal on its tricycle undercarriage. When I looked ahead I could see the ground ahead and not forced to look at the sky.

Brown settled into the rear cockpit and spoke over the intercom, talking me through the starting procedure. The engine emitted a discreet hum. A steady hiss came from whatever it was that pressurised the cockpit and we taxied out to the runway. Brown told me to put my hands lightly on the controls. 'Brakes on. Power on.' The humming rose by octaves, no vibration. Needles moved on their dials. No metallic clatter, just a high-pitched whistle as we rolled along the runway — walking pace at first, gathering speed — and WOW — suddenly airborne. Clunk, clunk (wheels retracting). We climbed towards the sun. At 15,000 feet Brown said the three words I'd been waiting for: 'You have control.'

This was it, living the dream. I was surprised how light those controls were — like driving a car with power steering for the first time, smooth, quiet. After seven minutes we were at 30,000 feet. It made me think of the heroic struggle that Edmund Hilary and Sherpa Tensing had in their conquest of Everest, a mere 29,000 feet, one year before. Brown again: 'If we have a flame out at this altitude we can glide for a hundred miles. That gives us a choice of four airfields on which to land.'

At nearly six miles above the earth Brown took control and immediately put the aircraft into a steep turn — first to the left, then to the right. He dived until the airspeed dial read 400 knots, pulled up into a loop followed by two rolls and a steep turn. My stomach wanted to evacuate itself in north and south directions but I was determined not to allow it to happen. I had already seen oxygen-starved Lubrano in a decompression chamber incapable of writing his name, so what would happen if my oxygen mask became clogged with vomit? I willed myself, swallowed hard and forced myself not to be sick while Brown continued to fling the aeroplane around the sky without relent. We climbed again. He put the aircraft into a near vertical dive and said, 'Mach One is the speed of sound, put your hands lightly on the controls, watch the dial and see what happens when we get close to it. I watched, gulping back sick as, right on cue, the aircraft began to shudder and shake and vibrate; it felt as if an invisible hammer was clouting the joystick.

'This is what happens at Mach nought point eight. Never try to go faster than Mach point eight-two if you want to see England again.' We climbed again and, before I realised what was happening, he had us in a dizzying spin, recovered, rejoined the circuit and landed.

Walking back to the crew room he said, 'Enjoy the flight, Stevenson?'

'Yes sir, absolutely tickety-boo as we say in England.'

However, something made me sicker than a dog a few days later that had nothing to do with flying.

Looking at my old log book I notice that my next flight was a full eleven days later. This gave some of us time to get invited to a 'Tom Collins' cocktail party in a nurses' hostel in the nearby city of Winnipeg where the roads were covered in packed snow blackened by rubber and oil. When the Tom Collins mixer ran out we eagerly resorted to pure gin, which made me extremely sick, so much so that I made an albeit short-lived vow never to touch Mother's Ruin again. In spite of this we made friends with the nurses and some of the civilian guests who lived in Winnipeg, but a few weeks later an unfortunate incident caused four of us to leave a drinks party by dashing for the door to save our lives — more about that later.

On 23 January 1954 Flying Officer Brown and I made two flights on the same day, the second included a GCA or Ground Controlled Approach, during which I wore a large opaque visor that stuck out from my helmet like a large sunshade — this forced me to look only at the dashboard. The GCA, sometimes called a Pipeline, was a brilliant way of getting pilots safely down through thick cloud or fog and well-trained operators in a ground-based radar station worked this magic every day, sometimes in clear weather to train people, sometimes in thick fog to save lives. Looking at a moving dot on two separate screens the operator sees if his customer is above the glide path, below it, to the left or right of it, while all the time speaking to his pilot with a speedy patter that would put an auctioneer to shame: 'You are above the glide path increase your rate of descent. You are on the glide path maintain your rate of descent. You are to the left of the glide path steer two degrees to starboard. You are below the glide path decrease your rate of descent. If you hear nothing from me after five seconds assume radio failure and maintain your height and heading.' And finally, if all had gone well: 'You are now one hundred feet above the runway, take over and land visually.'

After seven hours and forty minutes of dual instruction on a T33 Silver Star I was ready to make my first jet solo. During my six pre-solo flights, Flying Officer Brown insisted that at all times I should be aware of how G forces affect the human body. I was, after all, about to go alone in an extremely potent aeroplane (for its day). The T33 was a two-seat version of the Lockheed P-80 Shooting Star, America's first jet fighter in combat against Stalinist communism in far-away Korea throughout my time in Canada. My first flight had been in a Tiger Moth designed in the 1930s. Since then the calendar had moved on and aviation had become obsessed with the speed of sound, although only a few aircraft types were capable of exceeding it without breaking up. Fly too fast and an invisible wall of compressed air smashes the aircraft — and too fast for a T33 meant anything beyond 0.82 Mach (82% of the speed of sound). The problem was that the speed of sound becomes slower and slower the higher and higher you fly.

Portage la Prairie 2 Feb 1954

Dear Mother and Father
It is wonderful to hear that Ronald is now a lieutenant — I got a Christmas card from him yesterday (!?) with a photo of HMS

Ceylon *looking very spick and span.*

We are now at the jet school and flying the *T33 Silver Star.* In one and a half hours the aircraft uses *300 gallons of fuel and when full it weighs over 7 tons.* We have to dress up like men from Mars to fly this little motor and we wear two flying helmets — one made of canvas, which has earphones in it and over the top of that goes an enormous great white plastic crash helmet known as a bone-dome. Your face is almost completely covered by a large green oxygen mask; if you get an itch on the top of your head it takes quite a bit of time to scratch it — in fact it is much simpler to get someone to hit you on the head with a hammer!

I went solo for the first time in a jet on Friday of last week, 29 Jan and I felt a lot more confident than I was before my first solo in a Harvard. Everything went off quite smoothly with clear skies and sun shining. Four of us were up on our first solo trips at the same time and the Flying Control Officer was constantly calling us up in turn on the radio requesting our position and fuel contents. It was the first flight I had done on a completely clear day and from 30,000 feet the ground looked just like a map with Winnipeg appearing as a dark patch on the ground. Though Winnipeg and Portage are over fifty miles apart. I could see both of them without moving my head. Everybody goes solo between 7 and 9 hours.

The weather has really taken a turn for the better — when it got above zero Fahrenheit we thought we were having a heat wave, when it got above freezing we were sweating. The snow has started to thaw but the 'met man' is not too optimistic for the future, but it is certainly very enjoyable at the moment.

We take our final ground school exams next week — there are several new subjects including such things as Arctic Survival. I do hope I pass them ok as it would be grim to fail at this stage.

We watched the final practice for the Wings Parade of the senior course today. They will get their wings on Thursday then go by train to Montreal where they have ten days leave living on an RCAF base; after that they go to Halifax where they board a homeward bound ship, which takes them to Liverpool. That is probably what I shall be doing next month — NEXT MONTH!! — gee whiz does that ever seem like a short time! (still enough time to cultivate my English accent I think). My *estimated time of arrival home is between 20th and 31st of March — a revision of ETA will follow in my next letter but watch out if I arrive on the first day of the showery month! I am afraid I have just about run out of news because at the moment our lives are governed by the coming exams.*

I hope all goes well at Haughton-le-Skerne and that the winter is still as mild as ever.

Much love from James

Today is Friday 26 March 1954 and I am to be Number Three in a four-plane Finger-Left formation. It's been a busy day, two flights already because I'm cramming in hours before my final Formation Test due sometime next week (I'm nervous about it). Immediately after breakfast I had an hour and three-quarters with a rather verbose Flying Officer Brown, followed by another hour and a quarter flying solo in another formation exercise. Now I have to be Number Three, solo again, so there's a vacant seat behind me with no nagging instructor to bother us — would you like to come along? Here's your flying suit, your earphones, oxygen mask, plastic bone-dome. It's still cold. The sun shines from a cloudless sky. Melting snow wets our feet as we walk out to the most modern jet trainer in the world. You climb into the rear cockpit, strap yourself in and don't forget to attach the seat cushion to your parachute harness. I sit in the front cockpit and talk to you over the intercom. 'Throttle CLOSED, high pressure cock SHUT, battery switch ON.' I signal to the trolley-ac man to connect us to the external battery. I check that the fuel pressure warning light is ON and select fuselage tank pump ON. I press the starter switch for TWO SECONDS, we listen for the WHINE. I check that our fuel pressure light is OFF and the high pressure cock is OPEN. The jet pipe temperature is rising. The oil pressure needle shows a healthy 3psi and I signal our ground-crew attendant to disconnect his battery. We taxi out to the runway and form up behind the first two aircraft. We watch Leader (Johnny Cramb with instructor Paddy Cadogan) take off with Number Two (Sergeant Lubrano) tucked in close beside and slightly behind. If the runway was wider we could all get airborne together. Number Four (Lucky Lawson) is on the runway beside us, he is impatient as we are to get airborne. Now it's our turn. We have to catch Leader and Number Two and then close up in close formation. We start our take-off run but those guys ahead of us are disappearing into the distance at four miles a minute. We climb at full power. We close the gap. Soon we are looking into Leader's tailpipe and see yellow flames from nine blowtorches shoving him along with the power of two tons of falling bricks. We feel the twist from his jet-wash as burning air spirals back from his engine. We try to slide alongside Leader. We glance back at Number Four who's nudging our armpit. We look at Leader again, closer, closer — one false move and . . . TOO FAST — whoa, we're overtaking him — throttle back — still too fast. I flip the dive-brake with the little finger of my left hand but Leader goes sailing past us and Paddy Cadogan shakes his head in despair. We play catch-up all over again but this time I throttle back earlier and get in close enough to see scratched paintwork and an approving smile from Paddy.

After an hour of an Irish/Canadian voice telling us to use hand-signals, spread out into battle formation, turn right, turn left, cursing when we get it wrong, scatter, close up and reform, we are ready for Paddy to announce the grand finale: 'Tail chase in line astern, Number Three is leader.'

Number Three, that's us — and immediately we imagine that Cadogan, Cramb, Lawson and Lubrano are enemy fighter pilots trying to shoot us down. I push the throttle forward until it hits the stop. We turn tight and feel a burble that reminds me of the moment I flicked into an unexpected spin while dog-fighting a Harvard over Sylvan Lake. Turn the other way, burst through an isolated cloud, glance in the mirror and still the blighters are strung out behind us like a long twisty snake that won't let go. An idea sparks — it might just work, dangerous but who cares? I'm nineteen years old and so are you. We're immortal. We have three angry jets up our tailpipe. Let's disappoint them. Here goes, loop the bloody loop and lose so much speed at the top that they'll have to crash into us or swerve away. We start the loop, speed drops in the climb, hold the climb, sun in our eyes, keep climbing, slower and slower, controls go slack, slower — and, while we wobble on the brink of a stall why not tilt your head and watch an upside-down prairie slide up behind your back as we go over the top. After the loop we pull out of the dive and fly straight and level. The sky is beautiful, deep blue above the Perspex canopy. Scattered clouds below, bright under the sun — and we are alone, two miles up and nobody to play with. Feeling rather pleased with myself I press the transmit button: 'Where is everybody?'

Paddy answers from somewhere far away. 'You lost us, we didn't lose you.'

Now we can see the familiar triangle of runways. 'Look down, that's one of ours rolling to a stop at the far end of runway 27, and there's another on the glide — what a bunch of losers — ha, ha, ha. They all chickened out during our loop because they didn't want to bump into us.'

I must mention here an incident that happened at the end of a mass formation exercise with three separate finger-four formations all airborne at the same time before forming up into a twelve. I was flying with Flying Officer Scott in the back seat. Right at the end of the exercise Scott took control and we dived down to ground level over the airfield at well over 400 knots. Suddenly the aircraft began to porpoise up and down so violently that my bone dome repeatedly bashed the canopy above my head. I was taken completely by surprise and I can remember those brief seconds as if they happened last week. After we landed Scott said something about turbulence caused by the difference in temperature between the tarmac triangle of runways and the snow-covered ground between them — but I didn't believe him, and I still don't. My theory, for what it's worth, is that from his place in the rear cockpit he could see that my shoulder straps were slack and he couldn't resist the temptation to teach me a violent lesson by shoving the stick forward and back in quick succession thereby pounding my well-protected head against the Perspex canopy. From then on I made sure that my straps were tight before every flight.

Scott wasn't the only instructor to have fun at his student's expense as my Canadian friend Lucky Lawson discovered to his cost. Pulling G in a tight turn, when looping the loop or pulling out of a dive drains blood away from the head. The first symptom, caused by the optic nerve being starved of blood, is that everything goes grey. The second symptom is blackout, like trying to drive a car with your eyes shut — you're fully conscious but you can't see. But ease forward on the controls, black turns to grey and you can see again — ask any fighter pilot. Now just suppose that while you're blacked out (but otherwise conscious) you go on pulling more G in a turn or loop, so tight that your heart can't pump hard enough against the increased gravity — your blood-starved brain switches off and you pass out. Lucky Lawson was a six-foot-something Canadian student. His instructor was a foot shorter. The distance between the heart and brain of a short person is less than that of a tall person and that makes a difference when pulling G. Lucky's exceptionally short instructor could stand massive amounts of G without so much as a greying of vision but Lucky, over a glass of beer at the bar, told me that his pygmy instructor had rendered him unconscious on no less than three occasions while performing aerobatics.

Researching into what happened to some of my old comrades in later life I was shocked to discover that Lucky's luck ran out soon after he was posted to a Canadian Starfighter squadron based in Germany. Out of 200 Canadian-built supersonic CF-104 Starfighters, 110 of them crashed (no wonder they were nicknamed Widow-makers). Flight Lieutenant Douglas Charles Lawson was killed when his Starfighter number 12798 crashed on 4 March 1966. His body lies in Choloy Cemetry near Meurthe-et-Moselle in France.

16th Feb 1954

Dear Mother and Father
Thank you very much for the letter — it sounded as though you were in high spirits in spite of the slushy conditions of roads (and probably the paths as well). I too have been wearing a large smile as I have now

passed all the ground school exams necessary for Wings, which is a three ton weight off my shoulders. All that remains for me now is the task of flying as though I was reared in a rookery; unfortunately we recently lost a Canadian chap for failing Ground School and an RAF chap for flying, it really is a pity considering how far they got. The aerodrome was filled with navigators today as Winnipeg (where the Nav. School is) was fogged in. They use twin-engined aircraft (B25 American Mitchell bombers) as flying classrooms. One of them went off the edge of the runway while on its take off run — not exactly party manners but still.

I hope you like the Groupy when you go to Christina's wedding — it really is exciting. I hope I shall be at home for the next Guthrie marriage. What wonderful news about Ronald coming home. I do hope I see him and we get a decent bit of coinciding leave.

Continued 17th Feb.
We are just recovering from another cold spell. This afternoon, while sitting outside our hangar, it really seemed like Spring and the huge snowdrifts around the camp are shrinking away to nothing — it is of course very wet under foot. This course ends in

exactly four weeks from tomorrow but we will probably have quite a few days to kill while waiting for the ship to take us home. It will be good fun coming back by sea, and for most of us it will be the first sea voyage of any length. By the time we reach England we will probably be of the opinion that flying is strictly for the birds. I don't think I ever told you that Glynn Mills had a fire in their London office and consequently they are unable at present to send a full statement of mine or anyone else's bank a/c, in other words they are able to give the statement but without showing debits and credits etc to justify it unless specially requested.

There is not much more for me to say as not much seems to happen except flying. Yesterday I went low flying with my instructor, it was about the biggest thrill of my life — 500 knots at telephone-wire height certainly gives one a sensation of incredible speed. Love to all. I hope the animals are happy.

Love from James

Although I said that not much seemed to happen — what I should have said is that plenty of things happened that I preferred not to mention in my letters home. I could have told them about my bird strike, of which I was unaware until I climbed down after a solo flight and saw a long streak of blood stretching from just behind the nose of the aircraft and disappearing into one of the engine's air-intakes. I must have hit something big, like a Canada Goose — exactly the kind of bird (a flock of them) that caused flight 1549 to ditch in the Hudson river shortly after taking off from New York on 15 January 2009.

On another occasion somebody inadvertently pulled the wrong lever while his aircraft was stationary on the ground causing both wing-tip tanks to fall off; they ruptured and caused a 200 gallon flood of kerosene.

These incidents, however, are nothing compared to something far more serious. Having travelled from Montreal to Calgary by train we knew that Canadian railways consist of single-track lines interspersed with passing places at infrequent intervals. During that four-day journey we had admired our huge steam locomotive with its cow-catcher and forward-facing headlight. It must have been that headlight that put an evil idea into Mike Massey's brain because one morning he came into the crew room after a solo flight, unzipped his overalls and said casually, 'I stopped a train today.'

'Pull the other one!'

'I'm serious, the driver must have been shitting himself.'

Mike went on to tell us how, while flying at 20,000 feet, he saw the tell-tale plume of smoke from a train, chugging along its single-track. He flew in the same direction as the train, gradually losing height as he went, until he was about thirty miles ahead. He then made a 180 degree turn and brought his Silver Star down and down, lower and lower, until he was level with telephone wires. 'That's when the fun started,' said Mike. 'I opened the throttle and flew straight towards the oncoming train at 150 knots, slow enough to lower my landing gear.'

Somebody said, 'Why lower your wheels?'

'Landing-light of course — it's mounted on the nose-wheel fairing remember? I switched it on.'

Now we knew what Mike was talking about. As I listened to the unfolding story I imagined myself driving a train weighing thousands of tons and loaded with hundreds of passengers. In the distance I see a light coming towards me — it can only be one thing! I shut off the steam. I heave on the brakes with all my strength, but the oncoming train hasn't seen me. Do I stay with my train or do I jump? WHOOOSH — the light lifts off the single-line track, whistles over my cab and climbs away into the sky. The train stops. I am shaking. My fireman climbs down and vomits into the snow.

Mike continued to stop trains whenever the opportunity arose until, at a civilian party in Winnipeg, an unexpected encounter stopped him in his tracks just as surely as if he had been driving one of those railway engines. A group of us had been invited to a civilian drinks party in Winnipeg and it wasn't long before Massey, somewhat in his cups, attempted to enthral the assembled company by describing his by-now honed ability in stopping trains. By the expression on the face of a strongly-built man I could see that Massey's bullshit was touching a raw nerve, but the story continued unabated until the man suddenly barged forward, grabbed Massey by the lapels, shook him like a rag doll, gave him a tirade of obscenities and wrestled him to the floor. Massey freed himself, got up and led our group in a stampede for the door. Driving back to Portage on snow-packed roads Mike said, 'How the hell was I supposed to know those nurses had invited a train driver to their party?'

On one memorable afternoon we assembled on the airfield (suitably muffled against the cold) to see with our own eyes something we had already seen on film. A Canadian De Havilland Otter aircraft, affectionately known as the air force's one-ton truck, came chugging overhead at a height of 1,000 feet. Screwing up my eyes against the sun I saw the side door open, followed by a series of parachutes. A large sledge landed undamaged, followed by two nurses, eight huskies and a doctor. Once safely on the ground the huskies were hitched to the sledge, the three medicos climbed aboard and went careering across the snow. We met them afterwards in the mess, all members of a Canadian search and rescue squadron trained to locate aircraft forced down in the northern wilderness. We also met the dogs.

Saturday/Sunday March 6/7 1954

Dear Mother and Father
First of all there is a revision of ETA. Our course has been extended by three weeks, which postpones our graduation and Wings parade until April 8th after that it depends on the ships leaving Halifax but I should be home before May 1 for sure. This morning I went on a solo cross-country flight of 900 miles along three sides of a triangle — I really felt like Christopher Columbus with my pockets full of maps although the trip only lasted for two hours and thirty

*minutes (now that I come to think of it,
C.C. did not have any maps).*

Christopher Columbus I certainly wasn't but
I'll always remember looking down at the
wilderness of northern Canada from my
speeding perch and seeing absolutely no sign
of human habitation, no roads no towns, no
evidence that human feet had ever trodden
the ground that slid below me. What would
happen to me if the nine blowtorches that
powered my Rolls Royce Nene Turbojet were
to suddenly choke and die? A sledge pulled
by huskies — but would they find me? It had
already been drummed into me that at thirty
thousand feet I was flying high enough to
glide for 100 miles. But if I had a flame-out
what hope would I have of landing safely in
the patchwork of forests and lakes that
extended to hazy horizons in every direction
as far as I could see? Search and Rescue
— and it was no wonder that they had been
programmed to show their skills before we
students were scheduled to make our one and
only long distance navigation trip over the
northern reaches. But just suppose that
Canadian Jet 21163 were to burst into
flames. To save myself I would have to eject. I
knew how to abandon ship but doing it at
minus 70 Fahrenheit and at a height where

there was hardly any air to breathe was — well, better not to think about it. Six miles doesn't seem any great distance, but at that height the air is very thin. There's not very much of it up there, barely enough to hold you up. The controls feel slack, rather like driving a car with a lot of play in the steering. The speed of sound at 30,000 feet is a lot slower than at sea-level. What difference does that make? Quite a lot as it happens. I had seen what happens to a T33 when it flies at Mach point eight — or eighty percent of the speed of sound, but at 30,000 feet merely letting the nose drop a little while studying a map or generally failing to pay attention, allows the needle to creep unseen to point-eight and everything starts to shake and shudder.

Two hours and thirty minutes seems a long time when there's nobody to talk to, but it gives you time to think. The Korean War came to an end seven months before this flight but it made me think about the reason why I had been sent to Canada and why I was now flying in very thin air over a wilderness. Nuclear war against Russia seemed imminent, but which side would make the first suicidal move? The whole world knows what happened when two atom bombs exploded over Japan, but what a price to pay for World

Peace. Ho-hum, maybe, maybe not, but now I had more immediate things to think about. The American ADIZ (Air Defence Identification Zone) is a strip of airspace along the border between the USA and Canada; all aircraft must identify themselves before asking permission to enter this sensitive zone. Any unwary pilot who ignores the rule will be bounced by three F86 Sabre jet fighters, urgently scrambled by the US Air Force to investigate. Suspicious blips on radar screens have to be identified when the world is on the brink of war, even if the blip turns out be a rookie pilot with a bad memory. The trio of Sabres would surround the offender, one in front and slightly above with the other two on either side to form a moving trap. Once on the ground the intruder would face interrogation.

Not to be outdone the Canadians had their own security zone called CADIZ. In order not to provoke an international incident it was therefore necessary to radio the ADIZ and CADIZ operators well in advance: 'Hello ADIZ, hello ADIZ. I am Canadian Air Force jet 163 requesting permission to enter your zone at 12.55 hours.' On my solo trip I realised that I would be entering the hallowed area a good ten minutes earlier than I had planned: 'Hello ADIZ, this is Canadian Air

Force jet 163. My revised estimated time of arrival in your zone will be 12.45 hours.' They seemed friendly enough, almost welcoming.

At the second corner of the triangle Canadian Air force jet 163 met Canadian Air force jet 139 (another RAF chap also solo) so we closed up and flew in a two-plane formation back to Portage. I passed my last flying test on jets last week but still have quite a few more between now and 8th April. Last weekend I went to Winnipeg and bought myself a pair of shoes — Winnipeg is a very nice city but it was very cold and even in the busiest parts there was snow packed down on the roads. I think it would be a very nice place in Summer. My nav trip this morning took me north-east to a place called The Paz and the country on the way there is absolutely dead for about 300 miles. There was not a sign of civilisation — no roads, no fields, no trees — just a lot of iced-up lakes and rivers.

I would very much like to hear what Ronald is doing and when he gets home. When do Hew and John start their holidays? I expect it will be at the beginning of April or thereabouts. The current joke of the year around here is the adventures of two instructors who decided to fly to Trenton one weekend in a jet. Trenton is in Ontario about 900 miles east of here. Unknown to them their compass was unserviceable and as the first part of their trip was above cloud they had no visual contact with the ground. As you can imagine they got hopelessly lost and finally had to land in St Louis in the United States, which is just about 900 miles south-east of here. At our mess dinner last week the CO presented them with the Order of the Bull — a cardboard medal about the size of a saucer. On it was engraved a compass showing east and west in the wrong places and an inscription: 'For pressing on -------- and on.' This proved a scoop for all the local papers and St Louis became famous overnight. The unfortunate instructors had to wear these medals every night for a week whenever they entered the mess, or else buy drinks all round.

Will be seeing you possibly next month. Love from James.

We were told that the T33 Silver Star had a 'ceiling' of 47,000 feet, which is just under nine miles above the earth, and we were encouraged to test this ceiling for ourselves. I quickly discovered that no two aircraft are exactly alike. Some T33 Silver Stars could fly as high as 48,000 while others would be struggling at 45,000. During the last stages of a climb to these altitudes the rate of climb gets slower and slower, the controls get sloppy and slow to respond, the atmosphere becomes thinner and thinner, the Rolls Royce Nene engine can find barely enough oxygen to keep its nine burners going until finally the aeroplane literally refuses to go any higher. Perhaps the most striking evidence of this was supplied by a short length of red string. Why string, what has string got to do with it? A simple piece of string provided the most uncomplicated aid to aviation ever devised. Attached to the nose of the aircraft it blows back towards the windscreen — if the string blows back off-centre it tells the pilot he's either 'skidding' or 'slipping' in a turn — and that's easily corrected by small movements on the rudder. At lower altitudes the string trembles in a 350 mph gale. When travelling at the speed close to the T33's ceiling, however, the string flops about as if wafted by a gentle breeze. I think of that string whenever I hear people talking about global warming and greenhouse gasses because, yes, I've been there and seen with my own eyes just how thin that layer of atmosphere really is. Dip a football into a bath of water and notice how very thin the film of water is when you take it out — just enough to wet the football, and that's how thin our atmosphere is in proportion.

More than fifty years later I was astonished to read about the Rolls Royce Nene engine's ironic history. In 1945 the company's directors were keen to sell their new baby to the Russians who at the time were desperate to improve the performance of their own jet engines. Wonder of wonders the British Board of Trade's president, Sir Stafford Cripps, gave a favourable nod and within weeks a Soviet version of the Nene was powering Russia's star fighter, the MiG-15, on its maiden flight. The infamous MiG went on to score heavily against the American F-86 Sabre during the Korean War.

For obvious reasons pilots need to keep a good look out at all times, especially fighter pilots in wartime. When we first arrived at Portage our chief flying instructor, Squadron Leader Tiger Mullen told us: 'If you're wondering why I wear a silk scarf around my neck when I'm flying it's because my neck would be red raw if I didn't. At Portage la Prairie we teach you to pilot jet fighter planes and one day, maybe soon, some of you will find yourselves in combat against our enemies. Our guests from the French Air Force will be well aware that they already have a fight on their hands in Indo China. OK, so I keep my head on a swivel because I'm looking around for the enemy and I want you all to do the same. Silk scarves are optional but keep a good look out for the enemy because I'll be making sure that you do just that.'

20th March 1954

Dear Mother and Father
Here is the latest revision of ETA, which is all very much in the air at the moment. Our Wings parade has been finally fixed after a lot of wild rumour to the 26th of this month, which is next Friday and at last I think there is a fairly good chance that I might be on it. At the moment however it is highly probable that we will be flying for one week after that to bring us up to date on formation flying. I expect it will seem like my first drive in a car with no L-plates. The 26th will be a day of celebration, apart from obtaining wings it marks the 1st anniversary of being in Canada. It certainly doesn't seem like a year, although some-times it seems like a good bit more. Our chief flying instructor — Squadron Leader

(Tiger) Mullen has had a brainwave to improve everybody's lookout while flying. He cruises around the sky looking for poor unsuspecting student pilots (preferably solo ones) and then comes creeping up on them from behind. If he gets in fairly close without you seeing he calls you up over the aircraft radio with a cheery 'Good morning — this is Cosine 1 — happy landings.' (Cosine 1 is his call sign so when you hear that you know it's the Tiger) When you land you find yourself donating 25 cents to his 'retirement fund'. His aircraft has no tip-tanks, that's how you spot him from a distance. Luckily I haven't been molested by him yet, touch wood, but he has already theoretically 'shot down' three people.

In the above letter I must have forgotten to describe what happened when I chanced upon the Tiger high above Manitoba's prairies. I was about to make an imaginary landing on a flat-topped cumulus cloud when a sudden flash of reflected sunlight caught my eye. I looked again and there he was, the Tiger, far away in his highly polished Silver Star sans-tip-tanks and flying away from me. Surely he couldn't possibly have seen me. I immediately opened the throttle and gave chase. How sweet it would be, I thought, if I

231

could catch him up, get in close and then call him up on the radio with one of his own favourite greetings, like: 'Feeling kinda lonesome?' or 'Is your arse feeling hot today?' I imagined myself theoretically shooting him down and then inviting him to be the first to contribute 25 cents to my old-age welfare fund. I started to close the gap. He continued to fly straight and level probably in search of prey and without a care in the world until . . . Long before I could get close enough to claim a victory he flipped over onto his back and dived away.

Another of Tiger Mullen's favourite tricks was to secretly tag onto a four-plane formation knowing that at least one of the aircraft in the formation would be dual and therefore have an instructor on board. Looking out for the enemy in close formation is the responsibility of Leader because each one of his followers are staring at his neighbour and trying to stay alive by not bumping into him. Although it never happened to me, I heard graphic descriptions of how pilots in formation would suddenly hear in their earphones: 'Looks like fun, can I join in?' and then look round to find that the four-plane formation was now a five. But it wasn't funny, especially for the instructor who was no doubt torn off a strip in the privacy of Tiger's office while the students who hadn't opted to pay two-bits (25 cents) into his retirement fund were applying metal polish to his plane until it shone like silver.

This evening at 7 o'clock one of the Canadians on our course is getting married, so we are all going to the wedding. The C.O. is giving away the bride. There is a reception in town after the wedding, which should be good fun.

The weather is improving steadily and most days are sunny and cloudless but it freezes hard every night and there is usually a fairly strong wind. The other night we saw a wonderful example of the Northern Lights, it was just like a big arc of green and red light right across the sky — it was not nearly as clear cut as a rainbow and was much thicker and much longer and changing shape and colour in sort of waves — it really was a wonderful sight.

Love from James

In this letter I never mentioned the tragedy of 'Paddy's Night' scheduled for Wednesday 17 March. Flying Officer Paddy Cadogan was a Canadian/Irishman who returned to his home in Canada after serving with the RAF during the war. When the Cold War NATO Flying

Training Scheme appealed for flying instructors he rejoined the RCAF, stripped some rings off the sleeves of his old uniform and (as many of our instructors had done) rejoined the service at a lower rank. Paddy was a drinker (we all were), a raconteur of many a dubious tale and a thoroughly nice guy. By now I had flown 159 hours dual instruction and 62 hours solo and during that year some of the people I knew had been killed in flying accidents. Nobody talked about these deaths because only the eyewitnesses knew the details. To preserve morale no official announcements were made, but rumours would circulate: so-and-so is dead, but in some strange way I pretended that nothing had happened, convinced that no such thing could possibly happen to me — I was, after all, a teenager and therefore immortal.

Two days before St Patrick's Night the leprechaun borrowed an aircraft and flew 600 miles to see his mother in Vancouver, promising to be back at Portage la Prairie for Saint Patrick's Night. Paddy Cadogan was proud of his Irish origins and 'Paddy's Night' was going to be a great event. As soon as he was gone we set about decorating the mess with paper shamrocks, we collected Irish songs for the record player and somebody knew of a Winnipeg liquor store that stocked bottled Guinness and genuine Irish Whiskey. I ironed my white shirt and my black bowtie. I pressed my best-blue uniform and swallowed a brace of Alka Seltzers to prepare myself for Paddy's night but . . .

Paddy never showed. We were ready to start the evening. By ten o'clock we decided to wait no longer and the party went ahead with everybody asking the obvious question. The following morning, while helping myself to waffles and maple syrup, I heard how Flying Officer Patrick Cadogan had taken off from Vancouver after saying goodbye to his mother, climbed away on an easterly heading into the overcast and plummeted to the ground for no apparent reason. I could hardly believe it — Paddy the expert instructor, the immortal leprechaun, killed in a flying accident and nobody would ever know the reason why.

13

We were due for another spell of leave. Some cadets left the camp while others, including me, stayed put at Portage la Prairie. The stayers soon discovered that if they signed for an aircraft, people behind the desk wouldn't know that all trainees on Course 5303 were supposed to be on leave and not flying. What better opportunity could there be for a bit of illicit recreation, solo of course, no boring lesson plans to get in the way and no nagging back-seat drivers. Every day during that leave period the cloud base hung over us at around 5000 feet, but by now we had enough instrument flying experience to ignore sensations coming from the seat of our pants and climb safely up and through, provided of course we had each been given a 'penetration heading' from the control tower to prevent us from bumping into other aeroplanes while flying blind.

'Roger Bamboo two-nine. Cloud base five thousand. Your penetration heading is zero-seven-zero. Call one-thousand on top.' Bamboo 29 (my call sign) was now cleared to climb through cloud on a heading of seventy degrees magnetic, and when out 'on top' to radio back to say when clear of cloud. The controller always seemed pleased to know how high the cloud-top actually was and I suspect he was unaware that we were joyriding at the expense of NATO.

Waiting for take-off, before one of these flights, I hear two of my friends being given their penetration headings — obviously different to mine. I start the climb and within one minute become surrounded by thick black fog. I can't see a thing so I'm flying on instruments. Up I go until black starts to gradually change to grey, then to a lighter shade, lighter, brighter, brighter still, thinner and thinner until I burst out of the cloud-top into an eye-screwing dazzle from a sea of white foam below me as the aircraft rises like an arrow from the blanket. But what's that? Just as I'm pressing my transmit button to tell the tower that I'm one thousand feet on top, another T-Bird, like a great silver fish, leaps out of the 'sea' and climbs away towards the sun. I'm sorely tempted to give chase but a calming voice from inside my head reminds me what happened the last time I picked a fight with another aircraft.

On 5 April 1954 I passed my final formation flying test with Flying Officer Fink and knew that at last I would be on the graduation parade to receive the much-coveted flying brevet or 'Wings'. That date, however, turned out to be one of the blackest days in Canadian Air Force history.

While taking my formation test, another English trainee, 321 miles to the west of us, had just made a solo take-off from Number 2 Flying Training School and was climbing into the sky above Moose Jaw. It would prove to be Thomas Thorat's last flight; his Harvard crashed into the underbelly of a four-engine North Star. The Harvard's nine-foot propeller sliced through the airliner's fuselage, 37 people fell to their deaths and a woman on the ground was killed by flying debris. Local newspaper reporters guessed that Thorat must have been studying his map and never saw the airliner until it was too late. Newspaper accounts of the crash produced a string of complaints from Trans Canada captains who claimed that being buzzed by RCAF aviators was a frequent hazard of their job. Reading news of this horrendous crash reminded me of seeing North Star airliners at Calgary Municipal Airport, and my own disgraceful attempt at landing there. The North Star had been part of the Trans-Canada fleet since 1946, a fast airliner that could carry sixty passengers in pressurised and soundproof comfort over distances of up to 3000 miles in a single hop.

Tuesday 20th April

Dear Mother and Father

Thank you very much for the letter, it must be wonderful to have the daffodils out in the garden — surely that's conclusive proof that Spring has arrived. It is fairly spring-like here except for a very strong wind, which seems to blow most days. Here is the latest 'gen' — the Wings Parade will be on the 29th. We then proceed to Montreal by train where we ensconce ourselves in a ship called Empress of France. We expect to leave Montreal on 4th May and arrive in Liverpool on the 11th but I've no idea what time of day it will be. It will feel good to finally get our Wings after all the anxious moments caused by exams over the past year — and certainly wonderful to get home.

I stayed at Portage for my Easter leave and decided that I would visit the Hilley's on my way East next week if possible. False alarm about the spring weather, everything is covered with snow again after last night.

There was a bit of a panic yesterday — I went up solo on my last ever flight and found that I could not get my undercarriage fully lowered for my landing. The undercarriage indicators in the cockpit showed only the nose-wheel to be fully 'Down', the right main wheel 'Up' and the other main wheel 'Not Locked Down'. I radioed to the control tower and told them the trouble, then did a low pass in front of the tower so that the control officer could have a look at my wheels with his binoculars after which he said all three appeared to be down. Normally in this aircraft when, you close the throttle when your wheels are not down a warning hooter blows inside the cockpit in case you've forgotten to lower your wheels for landing. The hooter was blowing! The flying control officer then said he would get his 'little boys' out on the edge of the runway before my landing. The little boys, by the way, are the fire fighting crew and ambulance men. I was told to stooge around the skies to use up my fuel to reduce the subsequent bonfire and, with only ten minutes of fuel to spare I really concentrated on making a soft landing, not helped by a crowd of my friends who came out to witness a T33 belly landing on a collapsed undercarriage. Happily the undercarriage did not collapse and our chef provided me with a late lunch in the mess. The whole drama turned out to be a problem with the warning lights caused by a simple electrical fault. We have

*a mess dinner tomorrow and the speaker is
a chap who worked for underground
resistance movement in Europe during the
war, so it should be pretty interesting.
Longing to see you. I can hardly wait
— less than three weeks to go before I
arrive in England. Lots of love from James.*
   *PS. I hope there is nothing boiling over
in the kitchen.*

The after dinner speaker in question was a
young engineering officer who immigrated to
Canada after the war. He told us how
Denmark was invaded in 1940 by the Nazis
who attempted to install full military rule
over the population and issued orders that all
Jews were to be arrested and transported out
of Denmark to concentration camps hundreds of miles away. Due to some artful
undercover work by the Resistance nearly all
Danish Jews had fled to neutral Sweden
before the roundup could be organised. Our
speaker's stories of an illegal press, secret
drops of weapons from the air, sabotage,
derailments and factory fires gave me a real
feeling of what it must have been like — and
all this had happened less than ten years ago.
I can remember one of his stories in some
detail: sixteen year-old Edgar — let's call him
that because I can't remember his name

241

— received secret instructions to collect something from a house in Copenhagen and deliver it by bicycle to an address on the far side of town. On arrival at the pickup point Edgar was given a heavy parcel wrapped in brown paper and tied up with string. Far too big to conceal under his clothing, he fitted it to the carrier behind the saddle of his bicycle. Before setting off Edgar asked what the parcel contained and after some hesitation was told that it was a machine pistol. Edgar set off knowing that if he were stopped and the parcel unwrapped he would be forced to reveal his contacts then put against a wall and shot. Within minutes he was stopped by a German soldier who, after examining his papers, asked him the dreaded question. Trying desperately not to betray his fear and somehow managing a twinkle of humour, Edgar looked his questioner straight in the eye and said, 'That parcel contains a machine pistol and if you don't believe me why not undo the string and see for yourself.' After a moment of life-and-death hesitation the soldier laughed and waved him on. Edgar also told us how he dug flagstones from pavements, lugged them up three flights of stairs and dropped them onto Nazi soldiers and vehicles in the street below. While sitting there, listening to this man and trying to visualise what it must have been like to live in an enemy-occupied country, I suddenly realised that I was surrounded by Dutch and French friends of my own age who were probably trying to forget similar scenes that they had witnessed while at school. Edgar's talk sparked in me a life-long interest in wartime resistance workers. Characters based on these brave and unsung heroes are dangerous players in both my novels: *Fly the Storm* and *Dartmouth Conspiracy*.

Sunday May 2 1954

Dear Mother and Father
Thursday was the big day of the Wings parade — it is certainly a relief to have them sewn on my uniform at last. After the parade we had an elephant-sized party in the mess to which all courses were invited. The course below who are due to finish in 6 weeks time had laid on quite a programme for this party as it is common practice for the new senior course to lay everything on for the graduating course. They had made a most impressive archway around the door of the mess with the inscription: 'Thro' these portals pass the Greatest Jet Pilots in the World.' Quite early on in the evening our course

presented the *Chief Flying Instructor with a large china tiger (which I had bought)* The stretcher party who carried the tiger to the CFI's throne was made up of 2 RAF, 2 Canadians, 1 French, 1 Dutch. The tiger was supposed to represent the 'Tiger Spirit', which we had tried to live up to throughout the course — particularly appropriate as Squadron Leader Mullen's pet phobia is Tiger, Tiger, Tiger — every man a tiger. Rumour has it that he has stopped cutting his toe nails!

You may be wondering if I ever recovered from that party, but the real reason for the incoherent writing is that we are HOME-WARD bound in a swaying Canadian National railway carriage. We have been travelling since 4.30pm on Saturday and are scheduled to arrive in Montreal on Monday morning. We will sail from Montreal on Tuesday 4th in the Empress of France and, after calling at Quebec and Greenock, we dock at Liverpool on the 11th. We will all probably have to go to the Air Ministry in London as soon as we arrive and then return home for two or three weeks leave. Please just expect me when you see me. Longing to see everyone — it really seems like ages!

Just before the parade on Thursday, a Harvard bounced heavily to earth and out *popped Flying Officer Blaney and Flying Officer Riggs, two of my ex-instructors from Penhold. It was wonderful to see them again especially on such a memorable occasion. Neither of them had ever flown in a T33 and so they were taken up for a ride on Friday morning by two of the Portage instructors. Later that day they climbed back into their Harvard to start the six-hour flight back to Penhold — land of the ever-spinning propellers.*

There is not much more news to write about so I'll close this letter in the hopes that our next communication will be by word of mouth.

Love from James.

After a long train journey we arrived at Montreal. The ship towered above the jetty with bands playing and gangways bustling with embarking passengers. We found our cabins, came up on deck and were each given a narrow reel of tightly rolled paper. We then pushed in amongst civilian passengers crowding the rails and watched them waving goodbye to the crowd below and skilfully hurling the coiled end of their paper streamers to make a final link with loved ones on the jetty. I held one end of my streamer and threw the reel. A giggling woman caught it and held on tight as the ship trumpeted a last farewell. My final link with Canada untangled, stretched and finally broke as the ship edged away from the quay.

I remember wondering why the Air Ministry had decided to send us home by sea after having flown us from England to Canada in a BOAC Stratocruiser fourteen months before. I've since come to the conclusion that it was because of the British Overseas Airways Corporation's recent safety record. The De Havilland Comet, the world's first jet airliner, had been carrying passengers since May 1952 but had suffered no less than five disastrous crashes in less than two years killing 110 passengers and crew. The last two Comet crashes happened within four months of each other shortly before we were due to leave Canada. Both aircraft mysteriously broke up at high altitude over the Mediterranean and by the time I was safely on board our elderly Empress of France, all Comets throughout the world had been grounded pending investigation. An entirely new and strengthened version of the Comet took to the skies five years later. I believe that those last two disasters caused me and thirteen other expensively trained pilots to travel the 3,006 miles from Montreal to Liverpool across the Atlantic at a speed that would take us the best part of seven days.

Empress of France was the first ship to navigate the St Lawrence Seaway after the 1954 spring thaw. After casting off she was very soon accompanied by an iceberg-spotting Lancaster bomber from RCAF Coastal Command that circled over us as we proceeded north-east along the St Lawrence River and out into the warmer waters of the Atlantic Ocean. I was now a fully-fledged RAF pilot officer and Queen's Regulations & Air Ministry Instructions decree that officers should at all times travel First Class — be it train, plane or ship. So there I was, a nineteen year-old first class passenger on a prestigious transatlantic liner with wings on my uniform and in the company of good friends. I was literally floating.

The Royal Mail Ship *Empress of France* was launched from John Brown's shipyard on Glasgow's River Clyde in 1928 and christened *Duchess of Bedford*. Twenty-five years later, under her new name, she still retained an aura of decadent luxury from those elegant years of the roaring twenties. The old duchess had been around a bit; she had played a dramatic role during the Japanese invasion of Singapore during WW2 and later took part in the invasion of Sicily. Walking around the rail I noticed a brass plate describing how she had exchanged fire with a surfaced German U-boat and forced it to surrender. An elderly steward told us with some glee that pre-war passengers referred to the *Duchesses* of York, Atholl, Richmond and Bedford as the Drunken Duchesses for reasons we would soon discover.

Now rechristened, our empress sailed from Montreal at 1.24pm on 4 May 1954 and made her way up the recently thawed Saint Lawrence river, pushing her way through floating ice. After steaming for 139 miles, she passed the lights of Quebec off her port bow at 10.30pm before heading out into the Atlantic.

14

All the stewards on board ship were Liverpool men brimming with Scouse humour. During dinner, when I asked if the ship could travel at twenty knots, our waiter rolled his eyes: 'What do you think she is, a jet?' Every night we 'dressed' for dinner — not in the official RAF mess kit because we were only National Servicemen and the government had better ways of spending public money — but a white shirt and a black bow tie with best uniforms was different enough to give the civilian diners something to talk about. Unlike the reluctant ladies I had encountered at those Grantham Corn Hall dances, here there was no shortage of dancing partners. After dinner, on our first evening at sea, the dancing paused and we were entertained by a fast-talking comedian who made cracks about the RAF and sang this song.

I am a man as you can see, I'm not a girl, ha,
*   ha, hee, hee.*
Lots of medals I have won for brave deeds I've
*   never done.*
I'm an airman, I'm an airman, and I fly, fly, fly,

fly, fly,
Up into the sky, ever so high.
The sparrows cannot catch me however hard
  they try.
I'm an airman, I'm an airman, and I fly, fly, fly,
  fly, fly.

Starry-eyed applause from some of the ladies was punctuated with sardonic guffaws from a group of elderly gentlemen who looked suspiciously like retired brown-job colonels. We certainly had no medals but we did know how to fly, fly, fly, fly.

Later, at the bar, some old chap insisted on buying us drink after drink while tearfully telling us that the Battle of Britain had been won by youngsters like us and now, thirteen years on, Britain's aviation was going from strength to strength, striving for new records and creating new aircraft of revolutionary design that were being flown by chaps like us. That night I climbed into my bunk with a slightly sore and seriously swollen head.

Knock, knock, knock — every morning our cabin steward woke us up and drew back the porthole curtain. At 7.30am on our first morning at sea he told us that we were close to a place called Father's Point and if we got out of bed we would be able to see the river pilot climbing down a rope ladder to leave the ship, so we duly jumped out of bed to witness the event. On the second morning we were out of bed again when our steward falsely announced that a squadron of Catalina flying boats had just landed off the starboard bow. Every morning after that he made an equally dramatic observation calculated to induce Jack Wilkinson and me to spring out of our bunks and dash for the porthole so that he could get on with his bed making. Over the course of the following week we stoically ignored all further reports of early-morning mermaids, sea monsters, water spouts and many other wonders of the deep.

Leaning over the rail at the bow of the ship I watched pairs of dolphins leaping in and out of the bow-wave, diving, turning, chasing each other just as we had done in the sky above the prairies — a game of catch-me-if-you-can for the sheer joy of it. Were they doing these antics for fun — who knows? Flocks of Stormy Petrels danced on the water in their search for fish. And talking of fish, shoals of the flying variety would suddenly emerge from the waves and glide for long seconds before splashing back like handfuls of silver coins. Why? Because, we were told, the dolphins were hungry.

By the third evening all RAF personnel were trying to avoid a civilian passenger who seemed anxious to share his endless repertoire of dirty jokes. His glamorous wife had obviously heard them all before judging by her bored expression, including one about a sentimental man who at all times carried a lock of his mistress's hair inside his wallet and close to his heart. The punch line, I have to confess, brought a blush to my innocent cheek. This man, given half the chance, would go on telling his long-winded stories until midnight, when the lounge clock would automatically advance itself by one hour to mark our easterly progress.

After a few brandies I could usually persuade some of my RAF friends to go up on deck after dinner, face the wind and take the piss out of the Royal Navy by re-enacting scenes from a film we'd recently seen called *The Cruel Sea*. I would set the scene by gripping the rail with sea spray wetting my face, 'It's getting to be a different kind of war, Number One'. Right on cue Arnold Vick, dabbing salt water from his eyes, gave the never failing riposte: 'And the people in it are different too.'

At midnight on 11 May 1954 we arrived at Liverpool and the following morning watched a flight of Royal Navy Firefly aircraft buzzing the ship. I was sorry to leave the old empress but at the same time I was delighted to be back in England. After some rather serious interrogation by the Inland Revenue we cleared customs and were soon on a train bound for London. Every passenger was given a leaflet full of handy hints for the benefit of first-time visitors to England. One item in the leaflet informed us that the standard length of a rail in Britain was 60 feet and by using a watch with a second hand, one could calculate the incredible speed of the train by counting the number of beats per minute as the train sped over the joints. I can't remember the result of my calculations but I do remember that it was a whole lot quicker than the ponderous cow-catchers we knew so well.

Home life suited me, but not for long. Although my parents were at long last treating me as an adult and I was seeing a more relaxed side to them, my long awaited homecoming turned out to be something of an anticlimax. My parents were never very good at congratulating their four sons for modest achievements — perhaps for good reason — and after three weeks at home I was itching to resume my air force life. I was therefore delighted when a large envelope from the Air Ministry dropped onto the doormat, signed by my old friend the obedient servant; he had enclosed a rail warrant and was inviting me to report to Royal Air Force Station Oakington. Where was that? In the glove box of my father's Rover I found a road map of England and identified Oakington as a small village about seven miles south of Cambridge (the university I might have attended if I had been blessed with a better brain and had worked a bit harder at school). With the enclosed rail warrant I put on my uniform, bought a First Class rail ticket, caught the train from Darlington and, after changing trains en-route, found myself sharing a compartment with seven civilians. When a white-coated steward announced that lunch was being served, all eight of us duly proceeded along the side corridor to the dining car. In those days the dining area had tables for four on one side of a central gangway and tables for two on the other side. Being on my own the steward ushered me to a table for two already occupied by an elderly gentleman who seemed genuinely happy at having a companion to talk to. He put down his book entitled *Charles Dickens his Tragedy and Triumph* and we talked during lunch and for some time afterwards over coffee. On returning to my compartment I found my travelling companions in a state of mild excitement. 'Do you know who you were talking to at lunch?' I shook my head. 'Don't you watch television?' I shook it again because the last programme I'd seen on television was the queen's coronation. 'He was twisting his hair with his fingers, just like he does on the telly.' And finally they told me I'd been chatting to a famous man, a prolific poet and television personality later to become Poet Laureate. If I had known it was John Betjeman we would have had another topic of conversation as we had both been pupils at the Dragon School in Oxford up to the age of thirteen (missing each other by some 28 years). I had also missed seeing his TV series on British architecture so hadn't the faintest idea who I had been talking to.

An RAF driver met me off the train at Cambridge and drove me to Oakington to begin my new life as a fully-fledged Pilot Officer in the Royal Air Force. It was a reunion. All eleven of us had travelled from Canada on the same ship and the following day an official group photograph was taken of Number One Acclimatisation Course. After the photo we attended a pep talk from a Squadron Leader who failed to shock us with: 'Welcome back to Britain. How's cocksuckers country?' We later discovered that he had trained in Canada during the war and was therefore familiar with some of that country's quainter expressions. I can't remember what he said to us after that, but I do remember an unmistakeable atmosphere of jealousy shown by people on the station who had been trained from scratch in England and had not yet achieved their wings. What had possessed the RAF to allow the eleven of us miserable fellows to enjoy the Canadian Adventure?

My immediate impression of the Royal Air Force, after rejoining it, was of a service trying to ignore the blight of being the junior member of the three services, amongst whom the RAF was not always very popular. A naval friend of mine once told me that the only subject on which he and his father-in-law (a Brigadier) could agree was how dreadful the RAF was. For the past fourteen months I had been isolated from divisions of that sort, and also of the class distinction that was rife in England during the 1950s. I had been living in a country where snobbery didn't exist, where siblings from the same family might be lorry drivers, lawyers, dentists or dustmen and all of them on the same social footing.

However, as an RAF officer I had a room to myself and somebody to polish my shoes and wake me up in the morning with a cup of tea. When my batman first introduced himself I took a step back. It was none other than my old friend Stewpot who, under my instruction two years before, had become an expert at applying Blanco to RAF webbing. Somewhere along the line his dream to become a pilot had failed to materialize and now he was serving out his National Service looking after me, which made me think that the Royal Air Force must have been seriously overpopulated despite Stalin's nuclear threat.

On 11 June 1954, one week after my arrival at Oakington, I was issued with a valuable Omega wristwatch — an essential aid to navigation as the aircraft we were about to fly had no dashboard clock. I made my first flight in De Havilland Vampire T11 number XD387 sitting next to (not in front of) my instructor, Flying Officer Morgan. The Vampire was a small jet aircraft of unusual twin-boom design conceived during WW2 but born too late to face the Nazis. Compared to the Silver Star it seemed positively old fashioned with no power assisted controls, no ejector seat and an awkward system of wheels and wires to operate the trims.

Morgan warned me about Oakington's rather unusual main runway, built on a hill with the summit about halfway along. A take off run would begin with an uphill climb followed by an accelerating descent. The trick was, at all costs and on peril of death, not to ski-jump off the summit before flying speed had been attained, which meant easing the stick forward and riding down the far side of the slope until reaching 110 knots. After take-off, the first thing to strike me was the bustling landscape below, tiny villages by the dozen, irregular fields and a tangle of windy roads. Morgan told me to climb to 20,000 feet and show him some of the aerobatics I had learned in Canada. He wasn't impressed. The summer of 1954 was wet and cloudy for most of the time so flying often took place above cloud and out of sight of the ground with no roads, railways, villages, towns or coastlines to navigate by, and certainly no Rocky Mountains. Towards the end of a typical flight would often find me searching for a hole in a solid floor of cloud through which I could safely descend without bumping into other aircraft or going too fast. These holes were like small windows showing glimpses of gloomy East Anglia's landscape. The first time I tried to descend through one such hole everything began to shake and shudder. Morgan, sitting very close to my right shoulder, asked me what the hell I thought I was doing. What I didn't think or realise I was doing was pushing the Vampire past its critical 0.8 Mach and inviting the mysterious Sound Barrier to smash us to smithereens. Once safely under cloud, roads and railways below us were spread out like unravelled knitting with rain-soaked villages and a multitude of seemingly identical RAF bases adding to the confusion.

Oakington, however, had one — or should I say two — redeeming features to help rookies like me find their way home: the Old Bedford River and the New Bedford River, both twenty-four miles long and running parallel to each other, stretched in a south-westerly direction from Downham Market, about fifteen miles south of the Wash, to a village called Earith. Oakington's triangle of runways lay exactly six miles due south of Earith so once you spotted those 'Twin Canals' you knew where you were. My first flight with Morgan ended with a QGH, the RAF name for a ground controlled approach through cloud.

Exactly a week after my first flight with Morgan, I was ready to go solo having completed two hours and fifty minutes dual instruction on the Vampire — and it was a blessed relief to fly on my own without rubbing shoulders with my disapproving passenger. In front of me was a broad nose of aluminium acting as a visual reference against the horizon that helped me to put the aircraft into the slightly nose-up attitude required for landing.

Three days later I had a forty-minute sortie with Flight Lieutenant Hill-Turner, our squadron commander, who wanted to make sure that he could trust me with Oakington's one and only single-seat Vampire Fighter Bomber Mark 5. The cockpit of this fighter was tiny — in fact the whole aeroplane seemed much smaller because, like most modern cars, its snub-nose was invisible to the pilot. This would be my first, last and only flight in a single-seater. I walked out onto the tarmac with Hill-Turner who must have noticed the look of anxiety on my face because he quickly reassured me that the Vampire FB5 was a piece of cake. After squeezing into the cockpit and strapping myself in, Hill Turner assembled three or four attendant airmen to push down on the tail plane: 'A bit more, not too much, that's about it, hold it there.' He was a tall man. Standing to my left his face was almost level with mine. 'There you are Steve, that's the angle. See those trees? That's the view you should get just before touch-down. Good luck and for Christ's sake don't bend her.' I made a dangerous ski-jump of the summit of the runway and made quite sure I was well out of sight before rolling and looping this dainty little bird that, to me, would seem totally out of place in a serious war.

I needed my own transport. Courtier-Dutton had already bought an MG sports car and most of my other friends on the course had two-wheeled vehicles with names like Triumph, AJS, Matchless and Vincent. I remember thinking that so far I had avoided death, so why risk my life on a motorbike? An advert in the local paper caught my eye and after a perilous pillion-ride to Cambridge I inspected a well-used BSA three-wheeler dated 1934, being the year I was born, and therefore not very old. When I asked the dealer if it was reliable he replied, 'RELI-ABLE? I bought this car from a cripple. See that hand-throttle? He fitted that because he only had one leg. No self-respecting cripple would be seen dead driving an unreliable car.' I paid £60 and drove off.

My Dragon School friend Maureen Grieve was by now a student at Girton College. I hadn't seen her since we were twelve years old but I could picture us together on the narrow bench seat of my BSA, speeding off to a little place where we could share chicken in a basket washed down by a bottle of hock. Unfortunately for me she never answered my invitation.

After four new exhaust valves and re-wiring throughout, the twenty year old BSA reminded me of those horses at the Calgary Stampede — once going, hard to stop. I say once going because the battery tended to discharge when the car was at rest and cranking the engine with the starting handle had little effect. By far the best way to get the engine started with no friends around to help was to switch on the ignition, push the car to a fast walking pace, lean in, crash into third gear, wait for the engine to fire and then jerk the gear lever back to neutral. This became my regular routine until one day she got away from me, hurtled across the officers' mess car park, narrowly missed the Commanding Officer's Lagonda and came to rest in a stout hedge, thick enough to stop the car and stall the engine. Talking of cars reminds me of Oakington's very tall Meteorological Officer who preferred to drive his Austin Seven from the back seat with both front seats removed. His favourite passenger was a gigantic Saint Bernard bitch, his ever-loving and faithful companion, who would sit beside him. When seen from behind the dog looked exactly like a woman with beautiful hair.

RAF Oakington was a big station with large numbers of students who were doing all their training in the UK. Unlike us 'Canadians' they had not yet earned their Wings. Perhaps this was what made them try so hard to impress us with their knowledge of RAF traditions, most of which involved energetic after-dinner activities in the Officers' Mess while drinking beer to the point of nausea. Schooner Racing involved each member of a relay team rushing up to a table in turn, grabbing a brimming pint, downing it at top speed and sprinting back to touch the next idiot. On one particularly drunken night I witnessed the age-old RAF tradition of Footprints. For some inexplicable reason, foot printing graffiti across the ceiling of an officers' mess had infiltrated RAF culture during World War Two. It took quite a bit of doing and today the practice would doubtless be banned by the health and safety Gestapo. Imagine the scene — drunken youths chanting, 'Shoes off, socks off', and Imagine Pilot Officer Snooks set upon and forced to blacken his feet in a mixture of water and soot scraped from the massive stone fireplace; a table is dragged to the far corner of the room, Snooks is hoisted feet-first to the ceiling where he prints first his left foot, then his right to leave two Man-Friday style footprints on the ceiling. Next man up, footprints, down again, next, up, down — and wonder of wonders we soon have a trail of gravity-defying footprints walking across the ceiling and down towards the bar. These rowdy parties sometimes degenerated to a point where it was no longer funny. One poor chap was rolled up in a carpet, lifted onto the mantelpiece and left there until he begged for mercy.

I finished my flying on 5 July 1954 with

routine aerobatics and a high-speed run with Flight Lieutenant Woods. The following day I was awarded RAF Form 414 (A), signed by the officer in charge of flying training. Instead of marking me in the normal way as Exceptional or Above Average or Average or Below Average, I was assessed as Proficient as a Jet Pilot. I still have the document pasted into my log book. Looking back I'm convinced that Wing Commander Trent, hero of World War Two, complete with a row of medals that included the Victoria Cross, was kind enough not to blot my humble career with a shameful Below Average.

★ ★ ★

My flying days were now over. I had flown the Vampire, still wanted to be a farmer but had a further 59 days to serve before my two-year stint of National Service was up. Some of my friends had signed on for a further three years and were posted to operational conversion units to join squadrons on active service. I envied Courtier-Dutton who drove his MG to the RAF's research unit at Farnborough to become a human guinea pig before leaving to become a solicitor in civilian life. I stayed on at Oakington. After a spell with the controller watching Vampires ski-jumping off the brow of the main runway I was told to take charge of the control tower at Gravely, a small airfield about ten miles due west of our main base, used for practising circuits and bumps and close enough to relieve the pressure at Oakington. I travelled there every day with a driver and two airmen.

The main topic of conversation at RAF Oakington, and indeed Gravely, was something that was about to happen at London's Oval cricket ground on 17 August 1954. I've never shown the slightest interest in cricket, let alone test matches, but later that day I couldn't help hearing the buzz. In the control tower at Gravely my airmen were listening to the BBC on a portable radio with the sound turned down so that I couldn't hear what was going on — in any case I had other things to attend to with aircraft in the circuit for most of the day. However I soon discovered that England began the last day of play needing 43 to win with four wickets in hand, but the demon bowler Fazal was soon decimating the remainder of the English side. In due course Leading Aircraftsman Bloggs (I can't remember his real name) rushed up to me excitedly: 'They won sir, they won! Why not tell those Vampire pilots over the r/t? Go on sir, I'm sure they're all dying to know.'

I reminded Bloggs that if I did what he

suggested I would be disobeying Queen's Regulations and Air Council Instructions — but in spite of this I pressed the button on my microphone and said, 'They won.'

The reply from a pilot about to land was almost immediate. 'Who won?' At this point I decided to obey Queen's Regulations and say no more on the subject — because I hadn't the slightest idea which side had won and certainly wasn't going to ask Bloggs to enlighten me.

During my three months at Oakington we had two fatal accidents. A trainee from one of the 'English' courses crashed his Vampire into the North Sea. I didn't know the pilot and I don't remember any official announcement about it. No RAF funeral was held. I assume that his remains were recovered and sent to his home town for burial.

I get stark reminders of the second Oakington accident every time I go to an Italian restaurant. It happened during my final two months of service. A group of RAF Pilot Officers from Canada, who had not yet finished their acclimatisation course, invited me to join them for a meal at a small Italian restaurant in Cambridge. We sat at a table for six and drank Chianti while waiting for plates of something exotic called Spaghetti Bolognese. First question: how are we supposed to eat this stuff without it hanging down our faces and staining our clothes? The jovial *ristoratore* shook his head in mock sadness and came to our rescue: '*Fare una bobina con una forchetta e una cucchiaio.*' Luckily he had lived in England ever since his release from a POW camp and knew more than enough English to translate his advice into English. We watched in wonder as he skilfully coiled spaghetti into a tight bobbin, using the spoon as a mould, before popping into the nearest open mouth like a mother thrush feeding her chick. It was a great evening but my memories of it are sad. The following morning one of that group took off on a solo flight from Oakington, climbed into cloud and for some inexplicable reason nosedived his Vampire into a field. A female doctor, who happened to be married to one of our flying instructors, saw the crash, jumped out of her car, opened the cockpit from the outside and did what she could — but in vain. My friend was dead and I think about him whenever I see a spoon laid alongside a fork in an Italian restaurant.

Aircraftsman Second Class Stewart woke me up on the morning of Thursday 2nd September 1954 with a nice cup of RAF tea — it was to be my last, as this was my final day in the Royal Air Force. At breakfast in the officers' mess I checked the time on my valuable RAF Omega wristwatch (aircrew for the use of) and suddenly remembered that it belonged to Her Majesty the Queen. Unfortunately the officer in charge of wristwatches was on leave but after much persuasion the Adjutant agreed to take my Omega and return it to stores. I've lost the signed receipt so I hope they don't come looking for me.

I packed my suitcase, said a few goodbyes and drove home in my BSA three-wheeler. Although I was now a member of the RAF Volunteer Reserve and promoted to the rank of Flying Officer. I never wore my uniform again so didn't need to sew on the slightly thicker sleeve stripes. I was off the payroll anyway. The adjutant who took my watch had said, 'Cheerio Stevenson, you'll be in the Reserve until 1961 so if World War Three breaks out before then we'll send for you.'

My farming genes were still tugging. My next assignment was working on a farm in Scotland before studying for an agricultural diploma that led me to Portugal and changed my life — but that, as they say, is another story.

We do hope that you have enjoyed reading this large print book.

Did you know that all of our titles are available for purchase?

We publish a wide range of high quality large print books including:
Romances, Mysteries, Classics
General Fiction
Non Fiction and Westerns

Special interest titles available in large print are:
The Little Oxford Dictionary
Music Book
Song Book
Hymn Book
Service Book

Also available from us courtesy of Oxford University Press:
Young Readers' Dictionary
(large print edition)
Young Readers' Thesaurus
(large print edition)

For further information or a free brochure, please contact us at:
Ulverscroft Large Print Books Ltd.,
The Green, Bradgate Road, Anstey,
Leicester, LE7 7FU, England.
Tel: **(00 44) 0116 236 4325**
Fax: **(00 44) 0116 234 0205**

Other titles published by Ulverscroft:

DARTMOUTH CONSPIRACY

James Stevenson

September 1942: Luftwaffe pilot Karl Deichman must bomb the Royal Naval College in Dartmouth, despite knowing his cousin and childhood friend is resident there. Yet his orders give him no choice — the attack must proceed . . . After the war, Karl returns to England, haunted by the thought: *Did I Kill Andrew?* His quest leads him to a former secret agent, a wartime spy, and an ex-RAF Spitfire pilot; but as he uncovers the secret of the Dartmouth Conspiracy, he is drawn into a lethal trap. And it will be more than sixty years before the final jigsaw-piece falls into place . . .

FREDERICK DOUGLASS IN IRELAND

Laurence Fenton

In the summer of 1845, a man named Frederick Douglass disembarked ship in Dublin. It marked the start of a two-year lecture tour of Britain and Ireland by the celebrated author, orator — and escaped slave. Advised to leave America for his own safety after the publication of his eloquent and incendiary abolitionist memoir, Douglass proceeded to spend four months in Ireland describing and denouncing the horrors of slavery: packing full halls with his oratorical skill; sharing a stage with 'The Liberator' Daniel O'Connell; and taking the pledge from 'The Apostle of Temperance' Fr. Theobald Mathew.

THE BOOKSHOP THAT FLOATED AWAY

Sarah Henshaw

One day, a very strange business plan landed on the desk of a pinstriped bank manager. It included pictures of Cleopatra's barge and Ratty and Mole in their rowing boat — and petitioned for a loan to purchase a narrowboat plus a small hoard of books. Unsuprisingly, the application was rejected: undaunted, Sarah still succeeded in realising her dream of creating a floating bookshop. Captaining The Book Barge on a six-month tour of Britain's waterways, she is thrown into the deep end of waterborne literature retail: learning the intricacies of lock operation; bartering paperbacks for accommodation, bathroom facilities and cake; and rescuing stranded pigeons named Nelson . . .

WHEN FRASER MET BILLY

Louise Booth

Fraser was an autistic three-year-old boy, prone to anxiety and sudden meltdowns over seemingly the most trivial things. Day-to-day life in the Booth household was difficult. To Fraser's parents, Louise and Chris, the future looked bleak. But then Fraser met Billy, a grey and white rescue cat, and the two formed an instant connection. As Billy remained by his side, providing calm, reassurance and affection, Fraser made remarkable advances in his confidence, social interactions and contentment. Their profound bond brightens the whole family's lives — and has brought them many hilarious and touching moments along the way.

MUM'S ARMY

Winifred Phillips and Shannon Kyle

During the Second World War, young trainee nurse Winifred Phillips confided to her RAF boyfriend George Wheeler that she rather liked the idea of joining the Army herself . . . Enlisting in the ATS in 1948, she embarked upon twenty-two years' service in that and the WRAC, travelling the globe and reaching the rank of Warrant Officer Class Two. From dodging NCOs whilst eating illicit fish and chips, to dispatching invading snakes — and ultimately becoming one of the first two women to be admitted to the Royal Hospital as Chelsea Pensioners — this is Philly's story.